THE
WRONG STUFF

THE WRONG STUFF

HOW TO HAVE DISASTROUS DATES AND RIDICULOUS ROMANCES

DOUG PETERSON

Zondervan Publishing House
Grand Rapids, Michigan

The Wrong Stuff
How to Have Disastrous Dates and Ridiculous Romances
Copyright © 1990 by Doug Peterson
All rights reserved

Published by Zondervan Publishing House
1415 Lake Drive, S.E., Grand Rapids, Michigan 49506

Library of Congress Cataloging-in-Publication Data

Peterson, Doug.
    The wrong stuff : how to have disastrous dates and ridiculous
romances / Doug Peterson.
        p. cm.
    "Youth books."
    Summary: A dating guide that shows the right way to go about it by
first examining the wrong ways.
    ISBN 0-310-28721-9 (pbk.)
    1. Dating (Social customs) 2. Interpersonal relations in
adolescence. [1. Dating (Social customs) 2. Interpersonal
relations.] I. Title.
HQ801.P39   1990   90−36298
646.7'7—dc20   CIP
                                                    AC

All Scripture quotations, unless otherwise noted, are taken from the *Holy Bible: New
International Version* (North American Edition). Copyright © 1973, 1978, 1984, by the
International Bible Society. Used by permission of Zondervan Bible Publishers.

Edited by Lori Walburg
Design by The Church Art Works, Salem, Oregon
Illustrations by Corbin Hillam

Printed in the United States of America

90 91 92 93 94 / DH / 5 4 3 2 1

CONTENTS

Acknowledgments

First of all, I would like to thank the people who took time from their busy schedules to relate their disastrous date stories.

I'd also like to thank the girls who went on one and occasionally two dates with me in high school and college. You had incredible patience to put up with my Wrong Stuffness. Thank you, Melissa, Margie, Katie, Kelly, Debby, Maureen, Gail, and that blind date from another school who probably still has nightmares about our evening.

Also, a special thanks to all of the girls in high school whom I never dated but dreamed about dating—in particular, Sue, Cindy, Anne, and Danine.

Finally, thank you, Nancy, my wife. Thank you for making my dreams come true.

THE WRONG STUFF

In the 1950s, jet pilots first tackled "the sound barrier." With daredevil determination they drove their jets to the limits, trying to push past the speed of sound.

It wasn't easy. Whenever jets reached the speed of sound, strange things happened. Tom Wolfe reports in his book *The Right Stuff* that controls would freeze up. Jets would start rocking, shaking, and rattling wildly, spinning the plane out of control. Some jets even fell completely apart, tumbling in pieces to the ground below.

As I thought about those descriptions of hitting the sound barrier, I suddenly realized: Hey, that's a perfect description of my first date! On that and other awful dates I kept hitting a mysterious barrier, which I dubbed "the awkwardness barrier."

Whenever I reached this dreaded barrier, strange things would happen. My tongue would freeze up. The room would feel like it was rocking

feel like most of their dates have crashed.

Actually, though, I guess this book is about all of us. Even the most popular kids find that they crash sometimes. Even the popular kids can feel like they have the Wrong Stuff at some point in their lives.

I discovered the Wrong Stuff right from the start, on my first date when I went to pick up the girl and showed up at the wrong house. I went on to perfect the Wrong Stuff on future dates. At a movie theater I bonked my date on the side of the head as I tried to put my arm around her; then I bonked her on the other side of her head as I removed my numb arm. Later that same night, I tripped my way into a party, and then my extravagant gesturing knocked somebody's filled-to-the-brim glass across the room.

That was a blind date. Needless to say, I never saw the girl again.

I also had a date in which the girl said virtually nothing for the entire evening. And then there was the date in which the girl surprised me at the last second by bringing her girlfriend along. And then there was the date in which ...

You get the picture. So let's dive into the world of the Wrong Stuff, the world of dating disasters. To set the stage, we'll begin with step-by-step instructions on how to have a horrible first date, and then we'll take a brief overview of the history of dating. We'll even look at the first members of the world-famous Dating Hall of Shame.

So buckle your seat belts. It's going to be a rough ride.

and shaking and rattling wildly. The conversation with my date would go spinning out of control. And in most cases, I would see my evening fall completely apart and tumble in pieces to the ground below.

I had the Wrong Stuff.

This book is not about dating superstars who have the Right Stuff. It's not about those who have all the good looks and all the dates and all the popularity and all the attention. This book is dedicated to that large but noble class of kids who have the Wrong Stuff, the ones who

OFFICIAL WRONG STUFF GUIDE

Going On a First Date and Living to Tell About It

Phase One: Setting up the Date

1. Start to dial.

2. Chicken out.

3. Repeat steps one and two 452 times, then decide to call tomorrow.

4. When calling the next day, let the phone ring one-half time. Since no one has answered yet, they must not be home. Slam down the phone and take a deep breath.

5. Mope around for an hour and call again.

6. When your prospective date is finally on the line, tell her your name.

7. Stutter a lot when she says, "Aren't you the short, chubby guy with the smelly socks who sits next to me in homeroom?"

8. Tell your little brother to get off the line and to stop singing "I love you, I love you" in his Donald Duck voice.

9. Reading from a piece of paper, ask the girl to go out on a date.

10. When your voice cracks, tell the girl there must be static on the line.

11. Drop the phone and faint when the girl agrees to go on a date with you.

Phase Two: Preparing for Your Date

1. The week before your date, pass a love note to the girl at church.

2. After she opens the envelope and smiles at you, smile back.

3. During the offering, place your envelope of money in the basket.

4. A few minutes later, realize the envelope you placed in the basket contained your love note, while the envelope you passed to your date contained five dollars.

5. On the day of your date, try to hide your pimples by painting them to look like fat freckles.

6. Spend twenty minutes tying your tie nine different ways (skinny part too long, fat part too long, knot too wide, fingers caught in knot, nose caught in knot, etc.)

7. Throw away your tie and borrow your little brother's clip-on tie.

Phase Three: Meeting Your Date

1. Shake hands with your date's father and apologize for accidentally driving into the side of his house.

2. Shake hands with her mother and apologize for driving over her rose bushes.

3. Sit in the living room, across from her father, and wait.

4. Try to stir up an interesting conversation. Ask him, "Did you know that a cockroach can live for two weeks after its head has been cut off?"

5. When your date appears, show her the corsage that you had been storing in the refrigerator.

6. Suddenly realize you are holding lunch meat in your hands. Instead of the corsage, you mistakenly took a package of lunch meat out of the refrigerator.

7. Ask your date whether bologna would make a good corsage.

8. When she says no, place the lunch meat in your back pocket and rush home to switch the bologna with the corsage.

9. Return to your date's house and try to pin the corsage to her dress.

10. Accidentally pin your finger to her dress.

11. When her mother provides assistance, accidentally pin her mother's finger to your finger.

12. Ask whether a staple gun would be easier.

13. On the way to the restaurant, try to talk about things you have in common. For example, "Oh! I see that you have two legs and ten fingers! So do I!"

Phase Four: Dining at the Restaurant

1. While you wait for your friends to show up, hand your date's coat to a woman who looks like she checks in coats and hats.

2. Stare in surprise as the woman thanks you for the coat and ducks out the nearest exit.

3. To help your date get seated, pull out her chair.

4. Help your date get up from the floor after you forget to push the chair back in for her. Apologize sixty-three times.

5. Try to order food in French.

6. When the waiter gets furious at you, try to explain that you didn't know you were comparing him to a sick yak.

7. While waiting for the food to arrive, try to stir up an interesting conversation. Ask everyone, "Did you know that a cockroach can live for two weeks after its head is cut off?"

8. Place your foot against your date's foot under the table.

9. Become thrilled when she doesn't remove her foot. Maybe she likes you after all!

10. Leave your foot against her foot for an hour, even though your toes have gone numb and your ankle feels like it's about to fall off.

11. Become confused when your date excuses herself from the table and you still feel your foot bumping up against her foot.

12. After you realize that your foot has been bumping up against the table leg all of that time, massage your numb toes.

13. Bite into a piece of gristle and spend twenty-four minutes trying to get rid of it without grossing out everyone at the table.

14. Discover that the fastest way to get rid of gristle is to sneeze with your mouth full.

15. Find out that your meal contains very strong onions, which may explain why your date keeps burying her nose in her corsage whenever you breathe in her direction.

16. When you notice your breath beginning to peel the paint off the walls, eat four handfuls of mints from the dish near the cash register.

17. Try to be pleasant, cheerful, and agreeable.

18. When your date says she doesn't want dessert because she needs to lose weight, agree with her.

19. When your date clobbers you with a stale dinner roll, say, "Hey, no food fights. This is supposed to be a fancy restaurant."

20. Get a toothpick stuck between your teeth.

21. After the waiter leaves the check, realize that you accidentally put your wallet in the refrigerator when you went back to get the corsage. (The lunch meat is still in your back pocket, however.)

22. Ask the waiter if a slice of bologna would cover the meal.

23. Stall by acting like you don't know how the bill should be divided. Create confusion by saying, "Tom has to pay half for three-quarters of the chicken he ate, and Nick has to pay twenty-four dollars plus one-tenth of the tip, and Jim has to pay twelve cents for every one of my french fries he took, and Tom has to pay one-fifth of four-thirds of the bill, plus eight-ninths of the tip, which must be left in a brown paper bag at ..."

24. While everyone argues over the bill, rush to a pay phone. Ask your brother to bring your wallet over right away.

25. Finally pay the bill. But on the way out of the restaurant, let the door swing back in your date's face.

26. Realize that you forgot to hold the door open for her. Turn quickly, run into your date, and knock her into a decorative water fountain. Apologize twenty-six times.

Phase Five:
Driving Home

1. Try to think of something to talk about.

2. Try to think of something to talk about.

3. Try to think of something to talk about.

4. Panic.

5. When you pull into the driveway of your date's house, apologize for accidentally driving into the backyard. Tell her you thought it was a green driveway.

6. Realizing that you have pulled up beside a puddle (it rained the entire evening), run around the car, open her door, and place your jacket over the puddle, like a gentleman.

7. When she steps on the jacket, watch her fall into the puddle up to her waist.

8. Discover that the puddle was really a small fish pond, about three feet deep.

9. At the door, smile when she says, "God must have sent you into my life ..."

10. Slowly lose your smile when she finishes her sentence by saying, "... as punishment for my sins."

Phase Six:
Trying Again

1. Start to dial the phone.

2. Chicken out.

3. Repeat steps one and two 452 times and decide to call tomorrow.

4. Finally get the nerve to call her up and ask her for another date.

5. When she shouts, "NO!!" ask her to be more specific.

6. Tell your brother to get off the line and to stop making those kissing noises.

7. Hang up the phone, slink downstairs, and ask God, "Why me?"

8. Listen to your parents talk about Miss Crawfield, the church treasurer. They say she discovered a love note in the offering basket last week and has been walking on air ever since.

9. Smile. At least you made somebody happy.

THE HISTORY OF DATING

The Origin of Dating

Dating. Where did it come from? And why do we do it?

Was it started as a cruel prank by extraterrestrials who visited Earth millions of years ago? Or was it created by cavemen who were tired of sitting around the fire asking each other, "What do you want to do this weekend?" "I don't know. What's a weekend?"

Actually, neither one of these theories is correct. As the Bible makes clear, Adam and Eve were the first people to go out on a date. They had a blind date arranged by the Great Matchmaker himself.

Dates were simple back then. People didn't have to lay out sixty dollars on a deluxe dinner or fifty dollars on a fancy tuxedo, although Adam was known to rent a formal fig leaf from time to time. But there were still problems:

EVE: Adam, I've decided it would be better for our relationship if we saw other people.

ADAM: (glancing around) There are no other people.

EVE: Oh.

ADAM: So where do you want to eat this weekend?

EVE: You like apples?

Dating has never been the same since.

Primitive Dating

Back at the beginning of time, the world was filled with lots of slime and ooze, making it very similar to the dating scene today. The strange thing is that dating wasn't all that common in prehistoric time. Maybe primitive people knew better. Maybe they knew the pain involved with dating.

PRIMITIVE WOMAN: Hey, Spug, let's put these sticks through our noses.

PRIMITIVE MAN: And while we're at it, let's put hooks through our skin and hang from a pole.

PRIMITIVE WOMAN: Sure! And let's put huge disks in our mouths to make our lips stretch out a mile.

PRIMITIVE MAN: Yeah, and then we'll invent dating.

PRIMITIVE WOMAN: Dating? No way! What do you think I am, crazy?

Dinosaur Dating

Believe it or not, dinosaurs dated. But they had a history of disastrous dates, because meat eaters always tried to date plant-eating dinosaurs. Granted, the Tyrannosaurus

Rex was good about getting his plant-eating dates back home on time. It's just that his dates were usually in his stomach by the time he got them home.

The Tyrannosaurus Rex's biggest problem was his teeny-weeny hands, which made it impossible for him to put his arms around his girlfriend. This was very embarrassing and may have led to his extinction.

The Man Who Discovered Rejection

Grog Simmons, a Neanderthal caveman, asked Thilla Mogg out on a date to celebrate his discovery of fire. He got burned by both.

Dating in Old Testament Days

In Old Testament days, dating became very complicated. As you probably know, some men had hundreds of wives, so it's quite likely that they also dated hundreds of girls at a time. They called it harem dating. I call it harum-scarum dating. It sounds exciting at first, but can you imagine calling up hundreds of girls, buying hundreds of corsages, picking up hundreds of dates, facing hundreds of your dates' parents, reserving a table for three hundred, and getting them all home at the right time—all on the same night?

I think that's why men fought so many wars back then. It was more relaxing than dating.

Arranged Marriages

During ancient days, there were severe laws for everything. For example, double-parked cars were hung, not towed. And in dating, strict laws demanded "arranged marriages."

To arrange marriages, parents paired girls and boys together at age fifteen. This system gave parents total control over their child's romantic life. It also encouraged children to be very, very, very nice to their parents until age fifteen.

Date Inventions

The twentieth century saw the development of many great inventions, including inventions to help those who date. Here are just a few:

Boredom Canaries. In coal mines, workers used to check gas levels with canaries. If the canary died, that meant dangerous amounts of gas filled the mine. The "boredom canary" works on the same principle. The canary remains perched on your shoulder at all times during a date. But if it falls asleep, that means you are leaking dangerous amounts of boring conversation.

Velcro Lipstick. Quite handy for long kisses.

Acne Distractor. A Michigan inventor has the ideal answer for the girl or guy whose face breaks out just before the big date. The Acne Distractor is a balloon imprinted with the face of a person who has an even worse complexion than you do. Attach the balloon so that it bobs just above your head, and it will make your complexion look good in comparison. Your date may not even notice that you have a problem.

Shy-Busters. Does the idea of having a conversation with someone of the opposite sex strike terror within you? Then you could probably use a Shy-Buster—a handy tape recorder that straps to your forehead like a headband.

When you go on a date, just pop in a Shy-Buster cassette tape and the recorder does all the talking for you. If your date is also shy, both of you can wear matching Shy-Busters—just be sure to use the specially synchronized Shy-Buster cassettes so you can hold a conversation together. Shy-Buster Inc. offers cassette tapes that cover a wide array of discussion topics. There is even a special synchronized "argument" tape for couples who are too shy to fight.

Collect all fifty-four tapes and you will receive absolutely free the revolutionary "Shy-Busters Asking Machine." Use it as an answering machine in reverse. Simply program the machine to call a girl, saying something like, "I'm sorry, but Tom isn't home at the moment

to ask you out on a date for this Saturday night. But if you would like to go on a date with him, please leave your name and answer after the tone."

Today's Dating

Our historical overview of dating is complete. Now we turn from the past to examine the present and look forward to the world of dating in the twenty-first century.

In the past, rules of dating were simple. But changes in sex roles have made things a bit confusing. Here are just a few key questions:

Must the boy be the one who calls the girl, or can the girl call him? And should the relationship end if the girl's phone call is a bomb threat?

Should the boy open the girl's car door? Should the girl open the boy's car door? Or should they both sit inside the car and wave at people until somebody walking by opens their doors?

Finally, who should pay for the date? The girl? The boy? The bank? Or the person walking by who opened your car doors?

To answer the last set of questions, I suggest you examine this list of options:

 Traditional Dates—The boy pays for the girl.

 Dutch Dates—The boy and girl each pay their own way.

 Soviet Dates— The government pays.

Scottish Dates—Nobody pays.

 New Yorker Dates—The guy who mugged you on the subway pays.

 Californian Dates—The girl pays, but only if it feels right.

The Hazards of Dating

As you can tell by now, dating has many hazards. That's why some people prefer safer activities, such as rappeling down the sides of enormous cliffs using dental floss for rope.

The main reason dating causes so many problems is that we have a strange notion life will end if we haven't gone on a date by age sixteen. But that's not true. Life does not end unless you fail to get a date by age seventeen.

Ha, ha. Just kidding.

But that still leaves an important question. Where did we get the notion that dating determines our value as a person?

I don't know. Maybe we got the idea from that crafty snake back in the Garden of Eden. Maybe it was just the snake's idea of revenge. After all, the snake was probably jealous because he didn't have arms to embrace someone special. Nor did the snake have fingers to interlock with another's fingers. And the snake didn't have a hand to cover his mouth before sneezing all over his date, whom he was about to kiss good night. Dating may not always be Paradise. But it can be a highlight on the way to Paradise—as long as we don't take it too seriously.

TRUE STUFF

Chomp!

On the Trobriand Islands, if a woman wants to show a man that she is interested in him, she walks up to him and bites him.

Source: *Strange Stories, Amazing Facts,* Pleasantville, New York: The Reader's Digest Association, 1976.

Poof!

In northern Syria, if a man wants to show a woman he is interested in her, he blows smoke in her face.

Source: John May, *Curious Facts,* New York: Holt, Rinehart & Winston, 1980.

The World's Most Unique Christmas Gift

"Give of yourself this Christmas." In Sweden, some guys take this statement quite literally. They actually wrap themselves up in a box and have themselves delivered to their girlfriend's house as a present.

Source: *Reader's Digest Book of Facts,* Pleasantville, New York: The Reader's Digest Association, 1985.

Getting Drenched

Hungarians call Easter Monday "Water Drench Monday." On this day guys will keep splashing their girlfriends with water until the girls give them painted Easter eggs.

Source: *Reader's Digest Book of Facts,* Pleasantville, New York: The Reader's Digest Association, 1985.

The Invention of Dating

Dating is a rather new creation. In the United States, it didn't take over as the dominant form of courtship until the 1920s. Prior to that, "calling" was the main way to get a romance off the ground.

When a girl reached the right age, her parents would invite boys to "call" on her. And when the girl was somewhat older, she was allowed to do the inviting herself.

Calling was usually done in the home or at social events, under the watchful eyes of parents and neighbors. Dating, on the other hand, took courtship into the public arena of theaters and restaurants. There, surrounded by strangers, the boy and girl could enjoy privacy.

Another big difference is that with the calling system, the girl usually made the first move by inviting a boy to call on her. In dating, the boy has typically been expected to make the first move.

Source: Beth L. Bailey, *From Front Porch to Back Seat: Courtship in Twentieth-Century America,* Baltimore: The Johns Hopkins University Press, 1988.

Dating a Whooping Crane

If you think you're having trouble getting dates with a human being, try dating a whooping crane. It's no piece of cake either.

Just ask Dr. George Archibald—he dated a whooping crane back in the seventies. Why, you ask? Because when Dr. Archibald became interested in studying whooping cranes, there were only seventy-five of them left in existence. Therefore, scientists wanted all female cranes to produce more offspring by laying as many eggs as possible.

Unfortunately, a female crane named Tex was none too fond of the other cranes. So the scientists decided they had to artificially fertilize Tex's eggs with a hypodermic needle. Before her eggs could be artificially fertilized, however, somebody had to do a courtship dance with her. Because Tex liked humans more than other cranes, the job of doing a courtship dance fell on Dr. Archibald, director of the International Crane Foundation in Baraboo, Wisconsin.

So Dr. Archibald began to date Tex. Flapping his arms, bobbing up and down on his toes, he courted the crane most diligently. And it worked!

Once the eggs were laid, Dr. Archibald even helped the whooping crane by taking turns watching the eggs before they hatched. He straddled the eggs with his chair while he read or wrote. This freed Tex, the whooping crane, to go off and do her whooping crane chores.

Dr. Archibald was faithful too: he "courted" Tex every year for six years.

Source: Mark Jerome Walters, *The Dance of Life: Courtship in the Animal Kingdom*, New York: Arbor House, 1988.

No Coed Bookshelves Please

Some people went to extremes to keep males and females separate in England during the late 1800s. For example, Lady Gough's *Book of Etiquette* even suggested that books by male authors should be kept apart from books by female authors.

Source: Irving Wallace, David Wallechinsky, and Amy Wallace, *Significa*, New York: E. P. Dutton, 1983.

Chaperones

In polite circles of England in the early 1900s, chaperones were the norm when a boy and girl were together. Because a chaperone usually had to be married, there were sometimes cases in which a 35-year-old unmarried woman would be chaperoned by a 22-year-old married woman.

Source: Cecil Porter, *Not Without a Chaperone*, New English Library, 1972.

Dutch Dates

As you probably know, a "Dutch date" (or "Dutch treat") is when a girl and boy both pay their own way on the date. What you may not know is that this expression started out as an insult.

During the seventeenth century, the English and Dutch were fierce rivals. So the English did what many rivals do. They hurled insults at their opposition—the Dutch. A "Dutch concert" was their name for lousy music. A "Dutch nightingale" was a frog. A "Dutch bargain" was an unfair bargain. And a "Dutch treat" was when nobody treated. Everyone paid his or her own way.

Source: Tad Tuleja, *Curious Customs*, New York: Harmony Books, 1987.

If You Love Him, Fight Ants

If you think our dating system is painful, think about what the women of the Emerillon tribe in French Guyana go through before marriage (unless things have changed). To prove they are old enough to get married, they must lie in a hammock for five days and nights without food. But worst of all, they must fight off hordes of huge, biting ants. The local medicine man lures the ants to the hammock by putting down a trail of honey.

Source: Stan Lee, *The Best of the Worst*, New York: Harper & Row, 1979.

Whiskers in the Movie Theater

In the words of an anonymous civil engineer:

The school year was nearly over, and the big night had arrived. For weeks, I had been working up the courage to ask Annette out for the school's final "movies night." To my delight, she said yes.

In the foreign country where I grew up, "movies night" at the high school wasn't just any old date night. It was THE night for making new boy/girl alliances official and public. Annette wasn't your everyday date either. She and her twin were the blue-eyed, blond-headed darlings of every guy in the school.

My problem was shyness. Book work caused me no sweat, but dating was an altogether different story. I was sixteen, it was the end of my junior year, and I had never been on a "real" date (or, for that matter, on any other kind of date). The only reason I managed to work up enough courage to pop the question was the comforting encouragement I got from my bosom buddy, Jerry.

Jerry had been dating Annette's twin sister for several months, and he thought it would be "cool" if we two best friends could double-date the knockout twins. That way, he said, I didn't need to worry about what to do. I could just follow his lead.

Annette and I waited for her sister and my friend at the door to the movies. Time seemed to drag. I kept wondering what was keeping Jerry and his date. What was I supposed to talk about? When and how was I supposed to hold Annette's hand?

I wiped the sweat off my brow and tried to think of something to say to Annette. Then suddenly I remembered a conversation that I had had with Jerry a long time ago. In response to my complaints about my shyness around girls, he said that one day he would fix me up with the hottest girl in the school and my shyness would be no more. That's when I finally understood why he and his date hadn't shown up. To cure my shyness, he'd left me on my own with this gorgeous blond.

Because Jerry and his date never showed up, Annette and I ended up sitting next to a guy named Raymond, a somewhat reformed and very streetwise dropout.

With my eyes fixed on the movie screen, my mind raced to find an answer to the big question at hand: how to establish first contact? Obviously, most of the guys in front of me knew: I saw rows of draping arms and bent heads. When the movie was half over, I still hadn't even glanced over at Annette. The movie neared completion, and I knew it was now or never. Slowly, I lifted my arm and gingerly placed it around the back of her chair. Where I expected to find her soft shoulder in the darkness of the hall, I felt something strange. Whiskers.

Whiskers? For the first time since the movie started, I looked in Annette's direction. Raymond, the rascal, had made his move. He had Annette in a tight embrace, and they were completely oblivious to my presence. The whiskers belonged to him.

One day I shall bill him for her ticket!

Tony Campolo's Disastrous Date

In the words of Tony Campolo, sociologist:

I was the tough city kid, and she lived in the suburbs. I was an Italian ethnic, and she was a proper American girl. We met at a youth rally, and I was immediately smitten.

I knew some people who knew Judy and hence I could track her whereabouts from week to week. I knew exactly which church event she would attend, and I made sure to be there. I wanted to ask her out for a date, but I didn't know where to take her. Being a new fundamentalist Christian, I didn't understand the rules of the game. However, I knew enough to be aware that movies were out of the question and that dancing was a definite no-no.

One night at a youth rally, I was sitting two rows behind her, eyeing her. During the announcement time, the guy up front told us that everyone was invited to a Christian swim party. I wasn't quite sure what a Christian swim party was all about. I didn't know whether they prayed at them or preached at them or did some other spiritual thing at them. Anyway, I was a city boy. I grew up on the streets. I had never been in a swimming pool in my life. The only times I had ever been in water outside our bathtub were the once a year day trips our family took to Atlantic City.

In short, I didn't know how to swim. City kids dunk basketballs through hoops. They play stickball and stuff like that. I didn't swim and none of the guys that I knew ever did either.

But the guy up front said something that caught my attention. "This," he said, "would be an ideal date for Christians." There they were, the magic words—"an ideal date."

Not for a minute did I think my lack of swimming abilities should prevent me from going to this swim party. I'd just stay out of the water, sit on the edge of the pool, maybe dangle my feet in the wet stuff. I could even wade around the shallow end. I could bluff it. I could get by. After all, the guy said it was an ideal date for Christians.

As soon as the meeting was over, I moseyed over to Judy and pulled out my old West Philly High bravado. I came across as a tough, rough, urban, know-it-all. I did my best to impress upon her that I was the strong type who could handle anything. And then, in what I thought was a smooth move, I popped the question.

"Hey, what do you say we go to that Christian swim party together? I really think we could have a good time."

She said yes, and I was thrilled.

Finally the night of the big date came. We got to the party, which, incidentally, was held at a YMCA in downtown Philadelphia. There must have been a couple hundred kids there, joking and playing, shoving each other into the water and having a really great time.

Judy and I just sat at the edge of the pool—at the shallow end, of course. I told her about my heroics on the basketball court. I explained how my coach considered me the toughest guard ever to play at our school. I was acting like a true braggadocio when Judy said, "I'm thirsty. I'd like a Coke."

"Sure," I said. I helped her up and together we walked over toward the refreshment stand, which, unfortunately, was located adjacent to the deep end of the pool. As I was placing the order, two girls grabbed hold of my right arm. Before I realized what was happening, they had whipped me around and into the water.

The water closed over my head as I sank like a stone to the bottom. I panicked. Every time I bobbed to the surface I screamed and thrashed at the water insanely, but everyone just stood around and laughed. To them I was the "Macho Man." They thought I was just joking around.

Only Judy sized up the situation correctly. She dived into the water, grabbed "Macho Man" around the waist, and, using the skills that she had learned in her lifeguard course, pulled me to safety and out of the pool.

Let me tell you, it's tough being tough when a petite little girl has just dragged your limp body to safety. When the other young people realized what had happened, they reacted in various ways. Some laughed—I could handle that. But I felt like a fool when some others came over to tell me how sorry they were about the accident.

I dated Judy again, but it was never the same. After that date, she told me that she thought it would be good if we stayed friends. I knew what *that* meant.

The Man Who Didn't Know When to Quit

MORE STUFF

Ulrich von Lichtenstein, an actual, historic, thirteenth-century knight, epitomizes the ridiculous romancer. He probably holds the world's record in futility.

When Ulrich was twelve years old, he developed a major crush on a princess considerably older than he. He became a page in her court just to be near her, and some say he was so flipped out on her that he drank the water she used to wash her hands.

The princess never paid any attention to Ulrich, so he decided to impress her by becoming a knight. After many years of training, he finally decided he was worthy of her love. He composed and sang a song about her. The princess merely told him he was ugly.

Ulrich's next step was to have his face improved by a surgeon—an extremely dangerous choice in those days. After lying in a fever for six weeks after the surgery, he wrote another song for the princess, and she gave him permission to speak with her briefly at a riding party. At the party, however, he became tongue-tied while helping the princess from her horse, and the frustrated woman tore at his hair.

For the next few years, Ulrich fought battles in her honor, and he flooded her with letters of praise. She, however, flooded him with letters of castigation.

During this time, the princess became angry because Ulrich had falsely claimed to have lost a finger while battling in her honor. When Ulrich heard about her anger, he decided to make it appear that the story was true. He cut off his finger and mailed it to her as a gift. Some gift.

As his next stunt, Ulrich's friends announced that the godess Venus was going to emerge from the sea and joust with any challenger. Then Ulrich dressed himself up as Venus, pretended to walk out of the sea, and broke lances with hundreds of combatants over the span of several days---all in an attempt to impress the princess.

However, the princess decided she would not see Ulrich unless he disguised himself as a leper. She told him to join a group of lepers that was visiting her to beg for money. Dressed in rags, Ulrich spent a miserable rainy night with the lepers, huddled in a ditch. After waiting all night and most of the following day, Ulrich was finally summoned by the princess. She sent a message that he was to climb a rope up to her balcony.

Ulrich climbed up quickly, but when he reached her balcony she wouldn't see him alone. He persisted, and finally she told him that before he could be alone with her, he must go wading in a nearby lake. He agreed. But as he climbed down from the balcony, she untied the rope. Poor Ulrich plummeted to the ground.

He didn't die, though. After fifteen years of Ulrich's nonsense, the princess finally consented to give him her love—if you can call it that. Two years later she dumped him.

But Ulrich deserved it. After all, he had a

wife and kids during much of this time.

Source: Morton M. Hunt, *The Natural History of Love*, New York: Alfred A. Knopf, 1959.

The Couple That Kissed for a Real Long Time

In 1964, a Brazilian couple caused a traffic jam. While they paused for an embrace in their car, the braces on their teeth locked together.

Source: John May, *Curious Facts*, New York: Holt, Rinehart & Winston, 1980.

Group Dating?

There's something wrong with our system of dating, says sociologist Tony Campolo. He saw it himself in high school, and he still sees it today.

Tony first spotted the flaws in our dating system when he was president of his high school class and in charge of organizing a class dance. At the dance, Tony noticed hurting kids like Roger, who played disc jockey so he wouldn't face rejection on the dance floor. He also observed the girls who sat along the wall, waiting to be asked to dance and pretending they were bored. In

reality, many of them felt deeply rejected. Especially Mary.

Mary was a witty but not particularly attractive girl. In high school, beauty comes before wit, so Mary spent the entire night plastered against the wall, waiting to be asked to dance. That's all she did. Just waited. Tony tried to greet Mary after the dance, but she didn't answer. She darted for her father's waiting car. Safe in the darkness of the back seat, she broke down crying.

In his book *You Can Make a Difference* (Waco, Texas: Word, Inc., 1983), Tony said he was furious at the cruelty he saw that night. As he put it, "I saw some of my best friends and some of the neatest kids in our school getting hurt.

"Here is the real issue," Tony continues. "We have a dating system that glorifies the kids who are already glorified by our society and puts down the kids who are already put down. I feel bad for all the Marys of the world. I think Christians should be agonizing over what the American dating system is doing to people."

In his book Tony promotes group dating. Instead of pairing off in twos, guys and girls go out in groups of seven or eight. Exclusive dating does just as it says—it excludes. But group dating *includes* people and takes away some of the intense pressures of dating.

Tony says, "I wish you would make the following commitment: 'I am no longer going in for exclusive dating. I am going to foster group dating. It is all right for me to have a boyfriend or a girlfriend. But in social activities, I am going to make sure that everybody is invited, that everybody gets brought along, and that everybody participates. That's because it is a Christian obligation to reach out to the kids who feel left out.'"

You Are Not Alone

If it feels like you're the only one without a date this weekend, take a closer look. The February 1988 issue of *Campus Life* magazine reported a survey in which just half of the respondents said they dated once a week or once a month. The rest of the respondents said they either didn't date at all or else they only went on dates for the big events, such as the prom.

In other words, most people in high school and college are in the same boat. They do not date regularly.

2

THE FIRST TIME EVER I SAW YOUR FACE

When a boy and girl first meet, they act a lot like bats.

No, they don't hang upside down by their feet, although some girls may feel like stringing obnoxious guys up by their toes. What I mean is this:

When a bat flies, it beams out radar signals and then analyzes the return messages. That's how the bat knows when obstacles are in its path. In the same way, girls and guys constantly beam out unspoken signals to members of the opposite sex. Then they analyze the signals to find out how the other person is responding. It helps them to avoid running into obstacles to romance.

In his book, *Love Signals*,

David B. Givens goes through a whole list of unspoken signals sent out by males and females when they are looking for a mate. For example, if you unconsciously raise your shoulders or tilt your head down when looking at a girl or guy, you may be saying, "I'm not a threatening person. I'm OK."

Givens also says that when you are attracted to someone, you unconsciously turn your toes inward. And when you get excited about a person of the opposite sex, you tend to blink more often. You also may gaze at the person for a few seconds longer than normal, or you may unconsciously imitate the behavior of the person you're attracted to. In other words, you may cross your legs a few seconds after the girl or guy does.

Givens presents a whole grab bag of signals we send to each other in the early stages of a relationship, but he neglects to mention some of the more obvious ones. For instance, in my extensive research, I have learned that when a girl ties a boy's eyebrows to his locker, she is subtly telling him to get lost.

In high school and college, I was a real pro when it came to sending unspoken signals to girls. Just ask my wife. When I first met her, I decided to signal that I liked her by playfully stepping on her shoes—which may

explain why she had her entire Bible study praying that I wouldn't like her.

Fouling up your attempts to get a girl's or guy's attention (I mean *really* fouling it up) is what this chapter is all about. In the next few pages, we'll look at well-tested strategies for making that initial contact as awkward as possible. We'll analyze the fine art of worrying about dates—an important skill in the early stages of a relationship. We'll even look at many of the ways girls and guys try to attract each other's attention—with makeup, perfume, hairstyles, body language, and clothes designed to look totally stupid when you look through your old yearbooks ten years down the line.

If you're lucky, this chapter may even explain how to untie your eyebrows from your locker.

Trying to be Noticed by Someone Who Only Notices His Reflection in the Mirror

In Class

1. Glance at Seth very, very quickly.

2. Wonder if he noticed that you looked at him.

3. Pretend you are scratching the back of your head so it looks natural when you turn your head slightly in Seth's direction.

4. Quickly look at Seth out of the corners of your eyes.

5. Wonder if he noticed that you looked at him.

6. Drop a pen on the floor.

7. When you raise your head after picking up the pen, quickly look at Seth again.

8. Quickly look away because he saw you.

9. Try to act natural and cool by doodling on your paper.

10. Wonder if you'll be alive after your best friend realizes you just used indelible ink to doodle on her history paper—the paper you are supposed to turn in for her because she is sick.

11. Slowly turn your head in Seth's direction and look at him out of the corners of your eyes.

12. Wonder if you can break your eyeballs by moving them too far to the left. Wonder if they'll keep moving until you're looking at the inside of your head.

13. Feel a cold chill when you suddenly realize that Seth is staring at you.

14. Lock eyes and feel yourself turning red. He's staring at you for more than three seconds! He's *staring* at *you!*

15. Suddenly realize that *everyone* in the class is staring at you. Mr. Gleason just called on you.

16. Tell Mr. Gleason you didn't hear the question because you were staring at the map of France on the wall.

17. Promise God that you'll read a chapter in the Bible

every day for a month if he forgives you for the lie you just told to Mr. Gleason. Tell God it was really, really important that Seth think you were staring at a map—not at him.

18. Tell God you'll even read Leviticus.

Between Classes

1. Walk by Seth's locker between first period and second period classes.

2. Pray to God that Seth will walk by so you can say hi.

3. Walk by Seth's locker between second period and third period classes.

4. Tell God you'll read *two* chapters in the Bible every day for a month if you can just see Seth and say hi to him.

5. Walk by Seth's locker between third and fourth period classes.

6. When you spot Seth, suddenly realize you're walking the halls ALONE. You don't want Seth to see you ALONE or he'll think you're unpopular.

7. To prevent him from seeing you, duck to the side and keep your back to Seth while you stare at the map of medieval England hanging outside Mr. Gleason's classroom.

8. Say yes when Mr. Gleason walks by and says, "You sure like maps, don't you?"

9. Tell God you'll read three chapters in the Bible every day for a month if he'll forgive you for the lie you just told to Mr. Gleason.

In Class

1. Make sure you walk into math class right behind Seth.

2. Rejoice when you are able to take the seat behind him!

3. For fifteen minutes, study the back of Seth's head.

4. Notice a flake of something white tucked in among some hairs on Seth's head.

5. Pray that Seth doesn't have dandruff. That would be soooo disappointing!

6. Tell God you'll read four chapters from Leviticus every day for a month if you find out it's not a piece of dandruff.

7. Wonder whether it's just a piece of fuzz in his hair.

8. Lean a little closer to get a better look.

9. Lean a little closer.

10. Sneeze on his shirt collar.

Between Classes

1. Convince your friend Jenny to walk with you by Seth's locker between fourth and fifth periods. That way, you won't look unpopular walking ALONE in the halls.

2. Wonder whether Seth ever goes to his locker.

3. Tell Jenny you'll treat her to a bag of french fries if she joins you in walking by Seth's locker between fifth and sixth periods.

4. Spot Seth walking in your direction!

5. Die on the spot when Jenny points at Seth.

6. Kick Jenny in the leg to get her to stop pointing at Seth.

7. Act as if Jenny were really pointing at the medieval map of England hanging outside Mr. Gleason's class. Grab Jenny's arm and pull her over to the map.

8. Panic when Seth walks over and says, "Boy, you're sure crazy about maps."

9. Think frantically of things to say.

10. Decide that you should at least say hi to him.

11. By mistake, say "Hoy" instead of "Hi."

12. Tell yourself 142 times, "How could I be so stupid as to say 'Hoy'?"

13. Feel like a total idiot for the next two hours.

In Class

1. As you walk to the last class of the day, wonder if Seth thinks you have a serious problem in social skills.

2. Pray that Seth didn't even notice that you said "Hoy" instead of "Hi."

3. Almost run into Seth as you walk into class.

4. Feel good when he suddenly smiles at you.

5. Feel not-so-good when he waves, says "Hoy" in a goofy voice, and starts laughing hysterically.

6. Sit as far away from Seth as possible.

7. Slouch.

8. Sigh.

9. Stare at the map on the wall.

The Worry Scouts of America

It was a typical day. I woke up, terrified of life.

For starters, I was afraid it was my turn to floss the teeth of our family's pit bull. I was also afraid I would never get rid of those strange crease marks that the pillow chisels into your face during the night. But most of all, I was terrified that someday, maybe very soon, I would be dragged out on my first date.

The whole process of dating terrified me. I was terrified that on the night I got ready for my date, my hair dryer would click into reverse and suck all the hair off my head. I was terrified of my date choosing a formal dress made out of army fatigues, and I was petrified that the corsage I bought would ruin her camouflage.

Yes sir, I was a true Worry Scout, through and through.

The Worry Scouts of America, as you probably know, is an organization dedicated to the fine art of worrying. While Boy Scouts learn to tie knots in rope, Worry Scouts learn to tie knots in their stomachs. The Boy Scout motto is "Be prepared." Our motto is "Be prepared for the worst." The Boy Scouts climb mountains. We, however, make mountains out of molehills.

This particular day was the day of the Worry Scouts' annual camp out. And as I  already told you, I was in good worrying form. I was well on my way to earning a "worry merit badge" in the "dating" skill category. In fact, I expected to receive the honor sometime during the weekend camp out.

Worry Scout troops usually avoid camping in woods because there are too many hazards. A rattlesnake could slither into your sleeping bag, a tree could suddenly fall upon you, or an eagle could sit on your head and wait for it to hatch.

That is why most Worry Scouts camp in the safest place possible—the emergency room of a local hospital. Not only is help a stone's throw away, but the beat-up magazines in the waiting room make good fuel for the camp fire.

Unfortunately, a few years ago our local

hospital denied us permission to camp in the emergency room—maybe because last time we camped out there we made a mess roasting marshmallows with the X-ray machine.

As a result, we had no choice but to camp in the woods. Of course, we chose a spot at the edge of the woods, thirty feet from the nearest subdivision.

My job was to put together our troop's Worry Scout first-aid kit, which is no ordinary kit. Among its basic items are 4,356 bandages, 11 gallons of ointment, 1 operating table, 1 heart-lung machine, 2 brain surgeons, and 4 nurses.

All was going well. I even succeeded in packing my knapsack with more worries than

clothes. That's because this was the first year I was taking part in the annual Worry Boy Scout/Worry Girl Scout party to be held on the last night of our weekend camp out. Should I ask Melanie Yikes to the party? Would she laugh in my face? Or would she laugh in my face and then stoop down and laugh in my feet too?

But then something so amazing happened that I just had to tell my fellow Worry Scouts. I decided to tell them about it on the first night of the Worry Scout camp out—the night we traditionally spend around the camp fire talking about our latest worries.

So we all gathered around the camp fire at a safe distance of four yards from its flames. Mort Smith, a new Worry Scout with a promising paranoid streak, started off the list of worries.

"I'd like to tell everyone that I'm really worried about this camp fire," Mort said. He stood up and peered all around into the

darkness. Then he whispered, "I have this funny feeling that a Soviet bomber on a secret mission is going to see the camp fire and think it is a military target."

Everyone looked at the fire, then stared up into the sky. You could tell Mort's worry was a good one, because everyone else started to worry about it too.

Then Greg Lewis told everyone he was worried that our usual practice of dousing our camp fire with seventy-three thermoses of water wasn't going to prevent a forest fire. He suggested that we hire a group of tap dancers to dance on the coals and stamp out any remaining sparks. Everyone agreed.

Next, as Kevin Chubbock started to tell people he was afraid that a group of well-

financed first graders was planning to take control of our economy, I decided to make my move.

I leaped to my feet; but when everyone turned to look at me, I suddenly wondered if I was doing the right thing. Hesitating, I gave everyone the official Worry Scout sign, holding my nervous, shaking hand in front of me. Then I cleared my throat and opened my Bible.

"Fellow Worry Scouts," I said, "let me read from the book of Matthew: 'Therefore, I tell you, do not worry about your life, what you will eat or drink.... Who of you by worrying can add a single hour to his life?'"

I could tell that my Scout Master was very worried about what I had just read.

"Fellow Worry Scouts," I continued, "today started like any day, well-stocked with paranoias and obsessions. I was especially worried about dating because, as many of you know, I've been wondering whether I should ask Melanie Yikes on a date. But when I read those verses, something hit me like a ton of bricks."

"Did you hear that?" shouted Greg Lewis, jumping to his feet. "A ton of bricks hit him! I knew that might happen to someone! Every time I go downtown, I'm afraid somebody is going to drop a ton of bricks on me from an office building, and—"

I interrupted and told Greg that I used "ton of bricks" purely as an expression. A disappointed look crossed his face. But this was nothing compared to the disappointed looks I received as I went on to describe what I had learned.

"Fellow Worry Scouts, it suddenly occurred to me that I spent so much time worrying about what *might* happen in the future, I made my life miserable in the present. I was more miserable worrying about whether Melanie Yikes would reject me than I

would be if I asked her out and actually got rejected."

Nobody said a word.

"Then a strange thing happened on the way to the camp out. Normally, I worry about my car getting run over by a steamroller gone berserk. But this time I didn't worry, and it felt good." Looking at their disbelieving faces, I said again, "It felt *good* not to worry."

Before I could say anything more, the Scout Master leaped to his feet.

"Stop!" he shouted. "Stop right there before you cause any more damage. Are you trying to tell us that you no longer plan to base your life on worries?"

Slowly, I nodded.

"You know what this means, don't you?" he asked. I nodded again. "And you're not worried about it?" I shook my head. So the Scout Master motioned me to come closer. Knowing what was coming, I braced myself as he ripped the merit badges from my Worry Scout uniform.

"We can't accept you as a Worry Scout anymore," he said. "I am truly sorry, for you were one of our best Worry Warts. Why, I remember the time you were going to help a little old lady cross the street, but you wouldn't let her cross until the traffic lightened up, which, I believe, turned out to be two in the morning." He sighed. "Those days are gone, I'm afraid. We will miss you, but be assured that our worries will go with you." He saluted me worriedly.

An hour later, I felt the cool night air skim across my face as I drove home, all the windows recklessly open, radio blaring as if I hadn't a care in the world, and Melanie Yikes by my side. Yes, I repeat: Melanie Yikes sat beside me, her hair blown to joyous confusion by the wind. I had rescued Melanie from her worries of not getting asked to the campout party. And I had rescued myself from the worry that she would reject me.

I had to admit, though, I still had some worries. Melanie did too—I could tell. I could tell by the nervous way she smiled at me, and I could tell by the nervous way I smiled back. I think we were a little worried—just a little—about dating. But at least we were no longer worried that the sky was falling.

Tonight, we only saw God holding it in place.

How Do I Love Thee? Let Me Measure Thy Face

In 1903, G. R. M. Devereux wrote the *Lover's Dictionary*, which recommended that you study the facial measurements of the person with whom you hope to have a romantic relationship.

For instance, Devereux said you should reassess the relationship if the distance from the corner of your date's eye to the middle of the side of the nostril is shorter than the distance from the side of the nostril to the corner of the mouth. These measurements mean the person is stupid.

So the next time you walk your date to the door, don't bother kissing her. Ask if you can measure her face.

Source: E. S. Turner, *A History of Courting*, New York: E. P. Dutton, 1955.

Hairy Heads

In the eighteenth century, some European women went to great lengths to attract men—hair lengths, that is. Before going out to a ball or soiree, they would spend most of the day propping up huge heads of false hair with wire.

In fact, their hairdos stood so high that some women had to kneel to get through doorways. And the weight of their hair was so great that many slept with their necks propped on wooden supports. As if that wasn't strange enough, some of the women reconstructed battle scenes and displayed them on their heads of hair.

Source: Bill Severn, *The Long and Short of It: Five Thousand Years of Fun and Fury Over Hair*, New York: David McKay Company, 1971.

Love Long Ago

If a man in Victorian England wanted to pursue a girl, he had several hurdles to cross:

—First, he would try to meet the lady through friends.

—If that failed, he would try to see her at church or during her morning walks.

—Without speaking about his feelings, the man would look for positive signs from the lady: a blush, a smile, a shy glance.

—If the man got these positive signs, he would write to the lady's father.

—If the man received an invitation to the lady's house, he would not visit too frequently. Also, he would dress neatly and simply, and he would be sure not to act as if he were part of the family. If his journey was hard, he would not complain about it.

—The man would not offer any gifts to the lady until they were engaged to be married.

—Preferably, a marriage proposal would be made in a letter. The letter would be mailed, not handed to her in person.

Source: E. S. Turner, *A History of Courting,* New York: E. P. Dutton, 1955.

A Hair-Raising Experience

If you're trying to impress your date with a really classy hairdo, how about trying this one? In the nineteenth century, a French man had such well-developed muscles in his scalp, he could make his hair stand on end. He could even make one patch of his hair stand on end.

Source: Bruce Felton and Mark Fowler, *Felton and Fowler's Best, Worst, and Most Unusual,* New York: Thomas Y. Crowell Company, 1975.

The Wide Eyes Have It

Some scientists have claimed that men

are more attracted to women with dilated (widened) pupils. In one study, for instance, men were shown the photographs of two nearly identical-looking, blond women. Almost all of the men indicated that the woman with widened pupils was more attractive, but they couldn't say why.

People in Renaissance Italy must have been well aware of this tendency, because some women at that time used a type of eye drop to widen their pupils.

Sources: David B. Givens, "Silent Sonar: Is He/She Interested?" *Chicago Tribune,* 12 December 1983; and Bruce Felton and Mark Fowler, *Felton and Fowler's Best, Worst, and Most Unusual,* New York: Thomas Y. Crowell Company, 1975.

The Great Mascara Mystery

When the author of *Imponderables* tried to find out why girls open their mouths when they apply mascara, people offered him a variety of theories:

—Opening the mouth helps girls concentrate.

—Opening the mouth is an involuntary reaction of the body.

—Opening the mouth keeps them from blinking.

—Opening the mouth relaxes muscles in the face, making it easier to apply mascara.

—Opening the mouth tightens muscles in

the face, making it easier to apply mascara.

—Opening the mouth serves no function and is a waste of time to discuss.

Source: David Feldman, *Imponderables*, New York: William Morrow, 1986.

No Designer Clothes For Me

There's at least one place on earth where keeping up with the latest clothing styles doesn't play an important role in courtship. Among southern India's Toda tribe, girls have two garments to last their entire lives. One garment is given to them as children; the other is given to them when they get married. I assume this means they wear wrap-around clothing that can be adjusted as they get older. For more details, check out the "One-size-fits-everybody-on-earth" department of K-Mart.

Source: Stan Lee, *The Best of the Worst*, New York: Harper & Row, 1979.

Tattooed Makeup

If you're sick of applying makeup every day, try what some women did in nineteenth-century England. They had their cheeks tattooed pink and their lips tattooed red. On second thought ...

Source: Stan Lee, *The Best of the Worst*, New York: Harper & Row, 1979.

Tan Like Me

At one time, pure white, untanned skin was considered desirable in a mate. Pure white skin showed you were wealthy enough to stay indoors and didn't have to work under the sun.

Today, the fashion is reversed in our culture. Because so much of our work today is done indoors, a tan is a sign of wealth. It shows that you have enough leisure time to lounge around outside and develop a good tan. In the Bahamas, perhaps?

Source: Tad Tuleja, *Curious Customs*, New York: Harmony Books, 1987.

Bigfoot Solution

If you're trying to attract a date but are embarrassed by your big feet, an Oakland woman has a solution. Companies that install new carpet should provide people with matching slippers, she says. That way, your slippers will blend in with the carpet and nobody will notice your big feet.

She even suggests that slippers be made to blend in with linoleum floors, concrete, and Persian rugs.

Source: Randy Cohen and Alexandra Anderson, *Why Didn't I Think Of That?* New York: Fawcett Columbine Books, 1980.

Television Braces

A flash of straight, pearly white teeth is sure to impress a guy or girl. But what about television teeth?

A woman once suggested that fashionable people install extremely small television sets along their teeth. Can you imagine the attention you'd attract by opening your mouth and revealing a row of Bill Cosbys?

It beats braces ... maybe.

Source: Randy Cohen and Alexandra Anderson, *Why Didn't I Think Of That?* New York: Fawcett Columbine Books, 1980.

Rating-Dating

Before World War II, your popularity wasn't determined by whether you found a steady boyfriend or girlfriend, but by the sheer number of different people you dated. It was called the "rating-dating" system.

The pressure to go out on date after date was so great, Northwestern University girls agreed among themselves that they wouldn't date on certain nights of the week. That way, they could study without worrying that they were missing a chance to increase their popularity.

Source: Beth L. Bailey, *From Front Porch to Back Seat: Courtship in Twentieth-Century America*, Baltimore: The Johns Hopkins University Press, 1988.

Piano Pants

In the late 1700s, humans were not the only ones to dress modestly. Pianos did too. Certain American ladies decided it wasn't right for a piano to display its exposed legs. So they made specially designed pants to cover the legs of their pianos.

Source: Morton M. Hunt, *The Natural History of Love*, New York: Alfred A. Knopf, 1959.

Betrayed!

In the words of Brad Roos, ministry coordinator:

When I was a junior in high school, hanging out with the crowd was the thing to do. You never decided anything on your own; you always decided with the group's help. One of the things my friends and I weren't sure about was whether or not to go to certain dances, especially whether or not to go with dates. This was particularly the case with the junior prom.

As the time for the spring junior prom approached, we all fervently agreed *not* to go to the prom. So nobody got dates. At least that's what I thought.

About three days before the prom, I found out that *all* my friends had arranged to go to the prom with dates. How could they have done this to me? I felt betrayed, tricked. So there I was, three days before the prom, trying to get a date for this dance, which I didn't even know if I wanted to attend. It was a real adventure.

I got on the phone and asked a girl to the prom. But she was already going. It was hard enough to call three days before the prom to ask a girl to a formal dance; it was worse to be turned down. But I was determined, so I

called another girl. No, she had already promised to go with someone else.

Should I ask somebody else? Of course! Now that my friends were all going to the prom, I *had* to go. So I called a third girl. She was already going with someone else. I asked a fourth girl. *She* was already going with someone else. I asked a fifth girl. And a sixth. And a seventh. And an eighth. And a ninth. Ten girls!

This was getting fun. I didn't even care any more if they said no. In fact, sometimes I was overly rude. I'd call up and say, "Hi, I bet you're not planning on going to the prom." Or I would be very cheerful and astonish them by not being terribly sad if they said no.

Eleven. Twelve girls. I was desperate. I had run out of names. I finally settled on asking the girl who sat two seats in front of me in study hall. I knew only her name and that she was a sophomore, a year younger. So she probably wasn't going to the prom.

I called her up and asked her. She was thrilled and delighted. I said, "OK, this will be fun. I ask only two things. *Please* don't fix your hair real fancy and please, let's just make it a simple time. You don't have to get an expensive dress."

So the night of the prom I showed up at her door, ready to pick her up. But someone opened the door that I didn't recognize. I was about to ask if I had the right house when I realized it was my date. She stood there in a red velvet dress with matching red shoes, her hair piled up in a huge beehive. The two things I had asked her not to do, she had done, and I barely knew who she was.

I reluctantly took her to the dance. Afterwards, we joined my friends at a party. We were having a great time until my date took off her shoes. Then we saw them: her *bright* red feet. She had dyed her shoes the night before and the dye had come off on her feet.

Embarrassed, I took her home promptly, vowing never to speak to my friends again.

The Wrong Impression

In the words of Elaine Mustain, homemaker and aspiring writer:

He was tall, thin, dark-haired, and wore glasses. He wasn't alarmingly handsome, but comfortably so. And he didn't just *look* intellectual; he *was* intellectual. He was editor of the college paper. His name was Grady, and I wanted desperately to have a date with him.

I knew—I really *knew*—that even though he was a senior and I a lowly sophomore, if he only had the chance to get to know me, things would click. He might even fall in love with me. I might even fall in love with him. After all, he was a serious Christian, had a sense of humor, enjoyed the pursuit of learning, and appreciated nature and the arts. He seemed like a good candidate for something more than a casual relationship.

At last he asked me out—to a football game.

I was, as they always say, ecstatic. I did, as they always do, dress very carefully, spend lots of time on my hair, do my makeup perfectly. And I thought a lot about how irresistibly clever and artsy and intellectual I was going to be. I was ready. I was *really* ready.

It was a perfect afternoon: cold, clear, snappy—the ideal day for a football game. When he picked me up, he looked happy. I knew I looked good, but not gorgeous. I was not the sexy type, but I looked good. At any rate, looking "gorgeous" was not where my real strength lay. It was in my head. This guy was a writer, and I figured if I was going to impress him, I'd better say the things a writer would appreciate.

Things like, "Isn't it a *wonderful* day, Grady? I mean, just look at the sky. It's such a clear, *wonderful* blue! It makes you want to leap up in it and fly, and just glory in its light and beauty, doesn't it?" Which is something like what I said when we walked out the door.

"It is a nice day," he replied.

I knew I'd have to try harder.

"Look at the fountain!" I cried as we passed the lily pond. "It has rainbows in it. Let's stop and look at it for a minute." We stood there. "I love the sound of water splashing. It makes me think of rivers and waterfalls and the ocean and swimming in the summer. There's something so—*beautiful*—about the sound of water."

He smiled. "You're right, there is," he said.

We walked on, and I knew something was wrong. Surely, this guy was capable of conversation. In fact, I'd had several rather interesting ones with him before. I thought that's why he'd asked me out.

I tried again. "Don't you love the way the wind blows on days like this? It feels so—*free*—the way it flings your hair around, pushes against your back, and tugs at your clothes. Like the world wants attention and insists on being noticed."

He smiled again. "Mmm," he said.

And so it went.

About the game I said: "They look like ants swarming down there, falling all over each other in such a senseless frenzy."

About the sunset: "Look at the clouds! Like fluffy piles of cotton candy, so intense and pink and beautiful!"

About the cold: "It's amazing how the cold sinks into you and freezes you through and through until you feel like a sculpture carved in ice."

About the wool blanket we wrapped over our legs: "Wool is such an *alive* fabric! It makes you think of all those sheep and shepherds and fields and hills and trees. It even scratches as if it were alive."

And what did he say about all of the above, and everything else I said? "Mmm." And "Oh?" And "Yes." And "I think so." Things like that.

Clearly our date was less than successful. I don't even remember what we did after the game. Went out for something hot to eat and drink, I suppose. It didn't really matter, because I knew The Date was over long before.

Grady never asked me out again, and before we ever reached the door of the dorm, I knew he wouldn't, and I knew why. I hadn't let him get to know me, after all. The person who'd gone out with him wasn't really me, and whoever she was, he didn't like her. And I couldn't blame him.

She *had* been awfully pretentious.

The Man Who Wore Too Many Sweaters

In 1977, an extremely small, skinny Italian student developed an attraction for large English girls. While dancing with an English girl, however, he suddenly fainted. Doctors discovered that he had been wearing seventeen wool sweaters to make himself look heftier.

Source: Stephen Pile, *The Incomplete Book of Failures*, New York: E. P. Dutton, 1979.

The Man Who Lost His Hair

People love to judge others by appearances. That is how stereotypes are born. Take, for example, the "Dumb Jock" stereotype. This is the idea that athletes have more strength than brains—the idea that athletes go around wearing varsity letters because they're trying to memorize the alphabet.

My theory is that the Dumb Jock stereotype had its roots in the story of Samson—a prime candidate for the Dating Hall of Shame. Samson was a biblical jock, if you ever saw one. He made Arnold Schwarzenegger look like Pee-wee Herman. He could obliterate a thousand men using a jawbone as his weapon, and he could tear a lion apart barehanded. He would have made a great middle linebacker.

But Samson had one flaw. He fell for a woman named Delilah. And when you're in love, your brain sometimes stops functioning. At least it did with Samson. Consider this.

A bunch of Philistine thugs hired Delilah to find out the secret to Samson's strength. So, while the couple was out on a date, Delilah said to Samson, "Tell me the secret of your great strength." Samson had the sense not to tell her, making up a story about how he would become weak if he were tied up with seven thongs that had not been dried. (By "thongs," he meant the bowstrings used for shooting arrows, not the things you put on your feet and flop around with at the swimming pool.)

That night, Delilah crept into Samson's room and tied him up with the thongs. Then she shouted, "Hey Samson, wake up! The Philistines are upon you!" Samson promptly woke up and snapped the thongs "as easily as a piece of string snaps when it comes close to a flame."

On their next date, Delilah was at it again, asking for the secret to his strength. But Samson still had some brains left in his head, because he didn't give away his secret. This time, he said that if he were tied up with new ropes that had never been used, he'd become as weak as a wimp.

That night, Delilah crept into his room once again, tied him up with ropes, and shouted, "Samson, the Philistines are attacking you!" Samson woke up and broke the ropes.

Now, around this time, it wouldn't have hurt if Samson and Delilah had seriously considered breaking up, or at least seeing a counselor. They had an unhealthy trend going in their relationship. It should have been obvious to Samson what Delilah was up to.

Unfortunately, when you're infatuated with someone, you don't always see the obvious. Samson didn't. On the next date, a similar scene occurred. And then, on the fourth date, Samson did the dumbest thing that has ever been recorded. He gave away the secret to his strength. He told Delilah that if she trimmed off his hair, he would become incredibly weak.

On their very next date, Delilah got Samson to fall asleep in her lap. Then she signaled to the barber, who was hiding in the closet. He leaped out and turned poor Samson into a very weak skinhead. Samson awoke to Philistines barging into the room. They dragged him away as a prisoner.

The Philistines paid Delilah a good deal of money to betray Samson. But was it worth it? After what she did to Samson, she probably never got another date for the rest of her life.

Would *you* date her?

Source: *Holy Bible: New International Version*, the book of Judges, chapter 16, Grand Rapids: Zondervan Bible Publishers, 1986.

The Obsession

In her book *The Obsession* (New York: Harper & Row, 1982), Kim Chernin tells of a friend who contracted a brutal stomach disorder. The pain was so intense, the friend couldn't sleep. She said it felt even worse

than the contractions of childbirth.

Finally, after a brief stay in the hospital, the cramps began to subside. During those few days of cramps, the woman hadn't been able to eat. But that was quite all right with her. In fact, when a nurse entered the room carrying a scale, the woman became downright thrilled. She bounded out of bed, hopped on the scale, and called out, "I've lost four and a half pounds!"

The woman told Chernin she wished she could say that she'd rather have the five extra pounds back if it meant avoiding the excruciating pain. But she wasn't sure she could say that.

Can you imagine it? For all this woman knew, she could have had abdominal cancer, and all she could think about was losing five measly pounds. That's just one striking example of how obsessed we've become with appearances.

Appearances always have and always will play a key role in dating and marriage. But our society has gone well beyond a normal emphasis on appearances, at least for girls. Our obsession with thin girls and women has become a demon in our midst.

Chernin's book also refers to a study of middle-aged women. According to the study, more than half of the women surveyed said "losing weight" was what they would most like to change about themselves. What was extraordinary, the study reported, was that most of the women were not fat. They were not even noticeably overweight.

The Bible has something to say about all this emphasis on appearance. As God reminds Samuel in 1 Samuel 16:7, "The LORD does not look at the things man looks at. Man looks at the outward appearance, but the LORD looks at the heart."

Let's hear it for the heart.

The Deadly "I Am's"

Mike King knew there were problems the first time he spoke to Alberta Williams, a neighborhood girl. When he said to her, "Well, I'se preaching in two places," he knew he sounded like a hick to this girl from a cultured Atlanta family. To Mike, that first encounter with Alberta clearly spelled disaster.

Mike's sister told him he wouldn't stand a chance with Alberta unless he received more

education. So Mike had himself tested for his academic level, only to discover that he was functioning at the level of a fifth grader.

But Mike was determined. With Alberta Williams serving as his inspiration, this twenty-year-old guy returned to school, sat with kids half his size, and worked like crazy. Alberta, meanwhile, went off to her world—the college world.

Before Mike finished his high school degree, he was back on Alberta's front porch, this time asking her if she would like to go "courting." To the dismay of her cultured family, Alberta agreed.

Now, let's go back to when Mike spoke those first disastrous words, which sounded so unpolished. At that point, he could have told himself, "I am a lowlife. I am a jerk. I am a fool to think I could date Alberta Williams."

Fortunately, he didn't fall into the trap of the deadly "I am's," as therapist David Seamands calls them. In the competitive world of dating, it isn't always easy to avoid this trap. It can be tempting for us to say things like ...

I am unattractive compared to the people I see in advertisements.
I am a below-average student.
I am worthless.
I am ordinary.
These are the deadly "I am's."

According to Seamands, only God has the right to say "I AM," because he never changes. We humans, on the other hand, are always changing, always developing. We should never limit ourselves with "I am" this or "I am" that, because we are always in the process of becoming.

Mike King was able to change, and he knew it. Instead of telling himself, "I am a hick," he said, "I am going to *become* an educated person."

It changed his life. It also changed the history of our country. Mike King and Alberta Williams eventually married and had a child. The child's name was Mike King, Jr., but the world knows him by the new name that his father later gave to him—Martin Luther King, Jr.

GETTING SERIOUS

In the previous two chapters, you should have learned all the necessary skills for making sure your dating relationship fizzles on the launching pad. But sometimes, things don't go as you planned. Sometimes, to your great surprise, the first date actually succeeds. Then the second date succeeds, then the third date succeeds, and then ... lo and behold ... you find yourself without any more money because dates are horrendously expensive.

This is also when one of you will probably suggest "getting serious," because when you're dating someone seriously, you can go on dates that don't cost

any money. For example, you can go to the park and romantically push your date on a swing until you accidentally push her so high, she flips over the top, swoops down from behind, slams into you, and sends you hurtling across the playground like a cannonball. This is especially common when cartoon people go on dates.

When things start getting serious, one of you will say, "I think we should agree to go out only with each other." To your date you sound noble and self-sacrificing, but you know this is no great sacrifice, because it took an unbelievable amount of effort to get just one person to date you

you. The chances of finding somebody else to date would be about the same as a team of wart hogs producing a rocket and flying to the moon.

But how do you know if your date really wants to become serious? To answer this question, I have devised a foolproof test:

Step One: Study the notes that your date sends to you. If they say, "I (drawing of a heart) you," then he or she probably wants to become more serious.

Step Two: Study the notes that your date sends to you. If they say, "I can't (drawing of a stomach) you," then he or she probably *doesn't* want to become more serious.

Getting serious has its dangers, however.

The greatest danger is that you may become so obsessed with your boyfriend or girlfriend that you neglect your other friends. This will put a strain on your friendships. In fact, when your friends see you coming, they may walk on the other side of the street just to avoid you. (Except when your friends are driving. Then they'll drive down the sidewalk, trying *not* to avoid you.)

Getting serious was a stage I could never reach in high school or the first year of college. All the girls I dated wanted me to remain "just a close friend." Even when I first met my wife, she sent subtle hints that we should remain friends. For instance, one Valentine's Day she sent me a card that looked like the valentines you send in second grade. Then she scrawled across the card in large, little-kid handwriting, YOUR FRIEND, NANCY. The word *friend* was so big, I couldn't miss it.

I caught on to other tactics as well. When I walked with Nancy, she made sure she was always carrying a purse, umbrella, or something in the hand closest to me. That way, I couldn't hold her hand. But she used her best elusive strategy on a date with another guy. To avoid getting kissed at the door, she started tap-dancing on her front porch, leaped on the railing and tapped her way into the house.

But like I said, no matter how many obstacles are put in your way, you may be surprised to find yourself getting serious. In this chapter, we'll look at getting serious, taking your date home to meet the family, ditching electronic distractions for a serious relationship, and a host of other stuff.

OFFICIAL
WRONG STUFF
GUIDE

How to Have Your Date Over for Dinner Without Renting a New Family

Instructions for the Girl's Little Brother

1. Greet your sister's boyfriend by saying, "Hi, Bob."

2. When the boyfriend says his name is Nick, slap your head and say, "Oops. I guess Bob was the guy that Jenny went out with last night. Or was that Tom?"

3. Shake hands with the boyfriend.

4. Tell him his hand is sweaty.

5. Tell the boyfriend not to put on so much deodorant. Tell him his sweat is probably having a hard time penetrating the six-inch layer of roll-on deodorant, and all of it is backing up inside his body and coming out his hands.

6. At the dinner table, ask your sister and her boyfriend when they're getting married.

7. Offer to sell the boyfriend a photo of your sister that shows what she looks like early in the morning when she isn't wearing makeup and her hair looks like it has been danced on by monkeys.

8. Tell the boyfriend that early in the morning, your sister's breath even smells like monkeys.

9. Ask the boyfriend to quit moving his sweat-soaked hands so much because their loud sloshing sound is making it hard for you to think.

10. Ask your sister and boyfriend if they are planning a traditional marriage or whether they're writing their own vows.

11. Get the boyfriend to laugh when he's drinking so you can watch the milk spray from his nose.

12. Tell the boyfriend to stop playing footsie with you. Lean under the table and show the guy's foot how to locate your sister's foot.

13. Ask the boyfriend why he takes such a deep, deep breath every time he takes a bite of the liver and onions that your mom spent so much time preparing.

14. When the boyfriend is looking in another direction, make googly-eyed, love-struck glances at him and kiss the air.

15. When the boyfriend tells a joke, laugh wildly for five minutes, fall on the floor, laughing; stagger around the room, laughing; and repeatedly slap your thighs, laughing.

16. Ask your sister and her boyfriend if you can be in their wedding party.

Instructions for the Girl's Mother

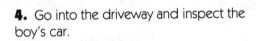

1. Inspect the boy's hair.

2. Inspect the boy's clothes.

3. Inspect the boy's shoes.

4. Go into the driveway and inspect the boy's car.

5. Check to make sure the boy doesn't have an earring in his ear.

6. Check to make sure the boy doesn't have an earring in his nose.

7. Ask the boy to sign a legal document that says, "I, _____, do hereby affirm that I typically dress and behave this way and am not just putting on an act to please Jenny's parents."

8. At the dinner table, offer the boy a second helping of liver.

9. Wonder why he hesitated and took a deep breath before saying yes.

10. Ask the boy what his father does, what his mother does, where they live, how they spend their evenings, whether he has a curfew, what kind of grades he gets, what his favorite subject is, whether he likes school, whether he has ever received a traffic ticket, whether he has a police record, whether he plays records loudly, whether he goes to Sunday school, what kind of movies he sees, whether he has cable TV, whether he has a job, what he wants to do with his life, whether he's going to college, what he's going to major in, whether he ever plans to raise a family, whether he saves money, what he spends money on, and how often he tells his mother, "I love you."

11. Remind the boyfriend that he should have Jenny back home by ten o'clock.

12. When the boyfriend jokingly says, "If Jenny isn't home by ten, will she turn into a pumpkin?" tell him, "No, but I'll turn your face into squash."

13. Offer the boyfriend a third helping of liver.

14. Wonder why he said a silent prayer before saying yes.

Instructions for the Girl's Father

1. When the doorbell rings, open the door.

2. Tell the boyfriend he has the wrong house.

3. Go back to reading the paper.

Romeo and Juliet in the Twentieth Century

(A Tragic Love Story)

Mr. Markus stopped at his office door, shocked speechless. The year was 1991, yet standing in front of him was a man dressed in sixteenth-century clothing, holding a sheaf of papers.

"I desire thy services, good man!" declared the visitor. "I am the famed playwright, William Shakespeare, and I have come to seek thy counsel."

Mr. Markus, a producer for the stage, rolled his eyes. Just what he needed—another looney who'd do anything to get on stage. But he decided to play polite anyway. "Yes, what can I do for you?" he asked.

"I have traveled to the twentieth century, faithful sir, to revise my writings. I seek to make them more relevant."

Make Shakespeare relevant? How many people hadn't had the same idea, and massacred Shakespeare in the process? Mr. Markus took the script and flipped through it. "I'll look at it," he said. "Come back later and I'll let you know what I think." With that he slammed his door.

After he'd settled himself at his desk, Mr. Markus picked up the script and began to read. It looked like a rewrite of the great love story, *Romeo and Juliet*. In the original version, the obstacle to Romeo and Juliet's love was their squabbling families. But in the twentieth century, the greatest obstacle to their love was something quite different.

This is what Mr. Markus read:

JULIET: (*She is standing on the balcony.*) O Romeo, Romeo! Wherefore art thou Romeo?

ROMEO: (*He is standing on the ground, wearing Walkman headphones.*) Juliet! Look below, for it is I, Romeo! With love's light wings, I will scale these balcony walls!

JULIET: Take care! If my family sees thee, they will murder thee!

ROMEO: What was that thou sayest?

JULIET: (*She speaks a little louder.*) My love, dost thou not hear my voice!? Or does the music of your Walkman fill thy ears to overflowing with noise?

ROMEO: Huh? What was that thou sayest?

JULIET: Take thy Walkman from thine head, so my words can reach thy ears and penetrate thy brain!

ROMEO: Rain? Why does my Juliet speak of rain when the night sky is as clear as the morning blue?

JULIET: *Brain!* I said *brain,* not rain! Remove that contraption from thine ears so we can talk until the morning is greeted by the lark!

ROMEO: Dark? Of course it is dark, my foolish Juliet. It is always dark at night.

JULIET: I said lark, thy silly bean brain! Doff thy headphones and—

ROMEO: Phone? Did thou sayest that thou hears a phone? Then I shall run and answer it! (ROMEO *exits as a frustrated JULIET bangs her forehead against a pillar.*)

Mr. Markus skimmed over the second and third acts. As the play progresses, Romeo and Juliet decide to date exclusively; but they rarely spend quality time together because Romeo prefers to fool around with his new personal computer. The only time they're ever really together is at parties where the music is so loud that they have to scream to hear each other.

One day, during a dispute with a rival over the rights to some software, Romeo accesses the guy's computer system and shuts it down with a computer virus. Before he flees to Barbados to escape the authorities, he manages to spend a final evening with Juliet.

JULIET: (*Tugging at ROMEO's sleeve*) My Romeo, thou must take flight! The authorities will be upon thee soon!

ROMEO: (*Irritated*) Be gone, nagging woman! Can'st thou not see I am watching the ball game? (*ROMEO adjusts the television set and munches on potato chips.*)

JULIET: But thou must flee, or I will never see thee again! Thou will be arrested and taken to the electric chair!

ROMEO: (*Rising to his feet*) O woe is

me, woe is me!

JULIET: What is it, my love? Dost thou hear the authorities knocking down the door?

ROMEO: O, it is worse! Much worse! The Cubs hath men on first and third, but they still hath failed to score! O woe is me! I will salt my potato chips with a stream of tears!

JULIET: (*Getting angry*) Thou art a fool! Ever since we started going steady, we never goeth out anywhere. All we do is sit in these chairs and watch sports or videos on thy silly boob tube. Thou never delightest my ears with conversation! A plague be upon thy TV set! I shall phone Friar Laurence to tell him my grief and seek his wisdom. (*JULIET rushes to the phone and dials.*)

PHONE RECORDING: Greetings. This is the wise Friar Laurence. As thou dost note, I am not home at the moment; but if thou desirest sweet discourses with me, leave thy name and phone number after the tone.

JULIET: (*Slamming down the phone*) A plague be upon his message recorder! Why is the Friar never at home? I talk with his recorder more than with himself!

ROMEO: (*Still glued to the TV set*) O, fair Juliet! Joy comes well in such a needy time! Ryne Sandberg hath doubled to left, and the Cubs hath a chance to win! What a happy day! What a—

(*Before ROMEO can finish his sentence, the authorities barge into the room and apprehend him. Then, after they all stop to watch the end of the ball game, ROMEO is dragged off and sentenced to life in prison.*)

In despair, JULIET yanks the antenna from the TV and falls upon it, killing herself. When ROMEO learns of her demise, he goes into a depression and decides to watch reruns of **Three's Company** nonstop for two days. *This poisons his mind, and he dies.*)

After the producer finished reading this tragic story, he wiped tears from his eyes and blew his nose. Just then a knock sounded on the door. Mr. Markus opened it to find William Shakespeare.

"I see thou hast read the script," said Shakespeare.

Mr. Markus pulled him into the office and seated him. "You're right, William, you're right!" he said, pounding his desk for emphasis. "Humans *are* more in love with their machines than with people! They let television come between them and the people they love! They spend more time with Nintendo than with—"

Suddenly the producer's voice slurred and his head fell forward, banging against his desk. A red light began to flash above the door, and his secretary rushed into the room.

"Is he all right?" Shakespeare gasped.

"Of course," the secretary said. "His battery just ran down. That happens to robots, you know."

Amorance Story

Many of the psychologists at the 1977 International Conference on Love and Attraction preferred to use the word *amorance* in place of the word *love*.

What is "amorance"? According to one of the psychologists, it is "the cognitive-affective state characterized by intrusive and obsessive fantasizing concerning reciprocity of amorant feelings by the object of the amorance, or OA."

Does this clear it up for you?

Source: John May, *Curious Facts*, New York: Holt, Rinehart & Winston, 1980.

Law and Candy Orders

In Idaho, it was once illegal for a guy to give a girl a box of candy that weighed less than fifty pounds.

Source: Dick Hyman, *The Trenton Pickle Ordinance*, Brattleboro, Vermont: The Stephen Green Press, 1976.

Will the Real St. Valentine Please Stand Up?

Who was St. Valentine?

According to legend, the Roman Emperor Claudius decided to abolish marriage because men weren't good soldiers once they got married. In response, St. Valentine secretly performed marriage ceremonies. He was murdered for his good deeds on February 14, A.D. 269.

Others believe that Valentine's claim to fame was helping persecuted Christians. For this work, he was thrown into prison, where he healed the jailer's blind daughter. On February 14, the authorities had him clubbed to death.

Source: R. Brasch, *How Did It Begin? Customs and Superstitions and Their Romantic Origins*, Longmans, Green, and Co., 1965.

Communist Love

According to reports, Communists in Burma were once advised *not* to tell their girlfriends or boyfriends, "I love you" or "You are beautiful." Those were not acceptable expressions. Instead, it was much better to tell your love, "I am deeply impressed by your qualities as a faithful and energetic member of the Party (Communist Party), and I wish to wage the Party struggle together with you."

Source: E. S. Turner, *A History of Courting*, New York: E. P. Dutton, 1955.

Shocking!

In America in the late 1800s, the *Ladies Home Journal* gave this advice: It is not proper for a man to stand at the gate of a lady's house for more than five minutes. This shocked some people who did not think a man should be allowed to stand at the gate at all.

Source: E. S. Turner, *A History of Courting*, New York: E. P. Dutton, 1955.

Love Adds Up

People have sung about love, they have composed poetry about love, and they have written countless stories and movie scripts about love. Now, love has even become a math equation.

A Harvard mathematician has devised an equation showing the changes in a relationship between a girl and a boy, whom he refers to as Romeo and Juliet. In this equation, the more Juliet loves Romeo, the more Romeo dislikes her. But the more Juliet dislikes him, the more attracted he becomes to her. As for Juliet, it's the opposite. The more Romeo dislikes her, the more she dislikes him; and the more he likes her, the more she likes him.

If that's hard to follow, then maybe the equation will help. It looks something like this: $dr/dt = aj, dj/dt = br$.

The next time you're inspired to stand beneath your girlfriend's bedroom window and sing love songs, forget it. Read math equations instead. It's incredibly romantic.

Source: Clarence Petersen, "As Usual, Boy + Girl = Confusion," *Chicago Tribune*, 30 March 1988.

The Love-Letter Champions

During World War II, Rev. Canon Bill Cook and his fiance, Helen, exchanged six thousand love letters over the span of four and one-half years.

Source: *The 1989 Guinness Book of World Records*, New York: Sterling Publishing Co., 1988.

A Kiss Every 6.48 Seconds

John McPherson, an Englishman, set a new world's record in 1988 by kissing 4,444 women in eight hours. That's one kiss every 6.48 seconds.

The *Guinness Book of World Records* doesn't mention any record for kissing the same person. If it did, the record might go to Sadie Nine and Paul Trevillion. They kissed each other 20,009 times in two hours. To train for such strenuous activity, Sadie and Paul bicycle, and they rub their lips with seawater and sunflower oil.

Sources: *The 1989 Guinness Book of World Records,* New York: Sterling Publishing Co., 1988; and John May, *Curious Facts,* Holt, Rinehart & Winston, 1980.

Kissing 101

At one time, the Open University of Washington D.C. offered a course on kissing. The course included instruction on the Air Kiss, the Dart and Dodge Kiss, and the Inhalation Kiss.

Source: John May, *Curious Facts,* New York: Holt, Rinehart & Winston, 1980.

Ankles Tell the Story

The 1950s saw the advent of the "Puppy Love Anklet." If you wore the anklet on the right ankle, that meant you were available. If

you wore the anklet on the left ankle, you were going steady.

Source: Beth L. Bailey, From *Front Porch to Back Seat: Courtship in Twentieth-Century America,* Baltimore: The Johns Hopkins University Press, 1988.

IN THEIR OWN WORDS

Look Ma, No Teeth

In the words of Greg Perkins, salesman:

The senior prom was a big event at my school, so I wanted to be sure to impress my date with how good I looked and how intelligent I was. So I rented the best tux I could find and spent an hour fixing the bow tie just so.

Finally the time came to leave. I drove over to my date's home and rang the doorbell. She came to the door.

I smiled.

She screamed.

"What happened to your front teeth?" she said.

I put my hand to my mouth. Sure enough, my false teeth were gone. I panicked. "They're gone!" I said. "But I think I had them in when I came to pick you up." We traced my steps back to the car, and there we found the teeth right underneath the car tire—only inches from certain destruction. I put them in—after washing them off, of course—and we proceeded to have a lovely date. Although, I did notice that my date kissed me quite cautiously that evening.

On another date, I lost my front teeth in the movie theater. I had taken my false teeth out during the movie to play with them—a bad habit of mine. But while I was playing with them, they got lost.

I said, "I've got to find my front teeth! I'm not leaving without them." So in the middle of the movie I hunted down the ushers, and we took out the flashlights and searched all over the theater until we found my false teeth.

You're probably wondering how I lost my front teeth in the first place. Well, in junior high school, I used to skip out of P.E. early so I could go "swimming" in the showers. I'd clog up the drains, turn the showers on full blast, and slide from one end of the room to the other on my belly.

I was having a fine old time—that is, until another guy decided to come into the showers the same time I was in there sliding around. I didn't notice he was in the shower until I slid into him, knocking him for a loop. He flipped, landing on the back of my head and smashing my face into the concrete floor.

So I grabbed my teeth (which had been knocked out) and ran out into the gymnasium. There stood a bunch of girls from the office. They didn't say anything. They just stared. I guess it's not every day you see a bloody-mouthed, buck naked boy run by.

Teeth to Teeth

In the words of an anonymous human being:

On the way home from a double date, my girlfriend and I were riding in the back seat of my friend's car. As we neared the driveway, I leaned over to give my girlfriend a

kiss. My friend, watching us in his rear-view mirror, slammed on the brakes. Youch! Our teeth clanged together. It was embarrassing, not to mention painful. In fact, although I never told my friend or girlfriend, they'd actually chipped a small portion of my tooth.

A Shy Prince Charming

In the words of Sharon, homemaker:

A girl's first date evokes feelings of excitement tinged with dread. In my case, the first date provoked more feelings of dread than anything else—for the date proved to be disastrous before it even began.

It was an October of mellow, vibrant days and cool, scintillating nights when a senior boy asked me, a freshman, to go to the first football game dance. My excitement grew with each passing day, but so did my dread. This tall, mysterious young man was even shyer than I was. This inspired me to plan a strategy.

In the solitude of my room, I put pen to paper, wracking my bashful brain, until I came up with a list of over twenty-five sincere, fascinating questions. All of them were designed to ease us both through the painful, silent early moments of our date and usher us through to an evening of lively conversation.

Armed with my list, which I soon committed to memory, I came to school confident all

would go well. That was two days before the *first date*. As classes ended that day, my tongue-tied Prince Charming met me at my locker, took the books from my arms, and said, "Can I walk you home?"

My house was nearly a mile from school, and we set out, trudging along in silence. As the silence grew more painful, I decided that perhaps I could spare a few of my questions for this "pre-game" date, as it were.

SHE: "Are you taking shop this year?"

HE: "Yep."

SHE: "Do you like it?"

HE: "No."

Hmmm ...

SHE: "Do you like movies?"

HE: "Yep."

SHE: "Have you seen any good ones lately?"

HE: "Nope."

Hmmm ...

SHE: "What does your dad do?"

HE: "Farms."

SHE: "Does he like it?"

HE: "Nope."

As the sidewalk stretched on forever before us, I went from question to question, running out of all possibilities long before we reached my front door. As the excruciating last moments dragged along in total silence,

my mind raced. I had depleted my entire supply of questions two days before the now dreaded date was to occur. If this walk home seemed long, that evening of sock-hopping would seem eternal.

My stomach continued to knot and reknot itself over the next thirty-six hours. So it is really no wonder that the night of the dance, the night of my long-anticipated first date, found me at home with a genuine bellyache.

Unable to go on the date, I breathed a sigh of relief. I've often wondered what my date thought. Perhaps he was equally relieved to have avoided the chatty little freshman who was so full of trite questions!

The Icy Empress

If you get nervous whenever your parents meet your boyfriend or girlfriend for the first time, be glad your mother isn't Anna Ivanovna, Empress of Russia in the mid-1700s.

It all started when Prince Michael Alexievich Golitsyn decided to marry an Italian Roman Catholic woman without the Empress's permission. The Empress was furious.

So what did she do? She constructed a palace, 80 feet long, 33 feet high, and 23 feet deep, and she constructed it *entirely out of ice.* The sculpture even included ice trees over 30 feet high complete with painted ice birds perched in their icy branches. The rooms contained furnishings made of ice, and outside a life-sized ice elephant spouted water 24 feet into the air.

Unfortunately, the Empress had a devious use for this ice palace. When the Prince's new wife died soon after the wedding, the Empress forced him to marry the most unattractive woman she could find. Then she paraded the newlyweds down the street in a cage and forced them to spend their honeymoon inside the freezing ice palace.

In the spring, the ice palace melted. The Empress died later in the year. As for the Prince and his second wife, they did more than just survive their ice-cold ordeal. They discovered they got along quite well; in fact, they lived quite happily ever after.

Source: *Strange Stories, Amazing Facts,* Pleasantville, New York: The Reader's Digest Association, 1976.

The Man Who Liked to Write Love Letters

A Taiwanese man once wrote seven hundred love letters to a woman over the course of two years. The letters worked: The woman married the postman who delivered all the letters.

Source: John Train, compiler, *True Remarkable Occurrences,* New York: Clarkson N. Potter, 1978.

Back to the Past

If you're starting to get serious with someone, let me forewarn you. Finding *true* love is a lot like becoming a two-year-old again.

During the first two years of life, a child has a strong sense of power. Who wouldn't? When you're an infant, all you have to do is dirty your diaper and people come running to your assistance. Want to be held? Cry. Feeling hungry? Scream. Adults will scurry around like circus clowns trying to figure out how to shut you up.

As children get older, however, they have to learn to cope with the real world, where people don't always jump when they cry. Some psychologists say this is one reason children go through what is called "the terrible twos." During the terrible twos many kids have a hard time dealing with the fact that they can't get everything they want. In desperation, they start ordering their parents around and throwing temper tantrums.

If you're beginning to wonder what all of this has to do with true love, I'll explain.

Psychiatrist M. Scott Peck notes that during the early stages of a dating relationship, a couple has a tremendous sense of power—just like an infant. They feel that their love can overcome any obstacle. This is the infatuation stage, when even the mention of your beloved's name thrills you.

Like a young infant, a couple that is infatuated with each other is not living in the real world. When you're infatuated with your boyfriend or girlfriend, you'll do almost anything to please him or her. You're on cloud nine. If your girlfriend asks you to juggle chain saws, you might even try it—just to see her lovely smile.

Let me repeat: This is not the real world. Most likely, this is also not true love.

The test of true love comes later, when the butterfly emotions have settled down. It comes when couples have to deal with nitty-gritty decisions of life together. It comes when you discover that your mate isn't going to do anything or everything to please you.

Like a two-year-old coping with reality, couples may have a tough time coping during this period. You may find your relationship plagued with quarreling and temper tantrums.

It's easy to act loving when your relation-

ship is new and fresh and exciting. But if you can act loving even when the emotional high is not so high, *that's* love.

Ask any two-year-old and he'll tell you it's true. Either that or he'll scream for twenty minutes.

Friday the 13th: What a Wonderful Day

In our house, we celebrate every Friday the thirteenth, because that was the day I first told Nancy I loved her.

At that point, we had been dating for about seven months, and the most romantic thing I had told Nancy was "You're great." But on Friday the thirteenth, I turned to her and said those words that sounded so strange coming from my mouth—"I love you." In fact, the words sounded so strange that I think I even said them in a strange way. Something like, "I luuuuve you."

Nancy's response caught me by surprise. She said, "Now, I don't want to scare you, but what exactly do you mean when you say you love me?"

This was interesting. She wanted definitions provided with my words of love. But not having a dictionary handy, I just stammered foolishly. Eventually I said, "Well, I mean I love you. You know."

Don't get me wrong. Nancy acted pretty thrilled about hearing me say, "I love you." She just wanted a little elaboration. Her next question caught me even more by surprise. She asked me if she had my rib.

"Huh?"

Nancy said she liked to think that her future husband was missing a rib. (Did she say "Husband"?) She reminded me that Eve was created out of Adam's rib. Eve had Adam's rib, so did I think she would have my rib?

Neither of us had had any X-rays taken recently, so I think I just mumbled something like, "Uh ... time will tell. Time will tell."

I'm sure I wasn't much help to her, stammering like that. But she *really* wanted to know what I meant by "I love you." And even

though it made me feel pretty awkward at the time, it was a good question.

You see, guys had told her they loved her before, and they often meant different things. It happens all the time. One guy might say "I love you because he's truly committed; he's ready to give his life for his girlfriend. Another guy might say "I love you" because he's been infatuated with the girl for the entire fifteen minutes he's known her. Another guy might say "I love you" because he wants to convince the girl to fool around sexually. And another guy might say "I love you" because he has been dating the girl for a while and it just seems like the right thing to say.

Nancy's question made one thing very clear to me: I tended to use powerful words very loosely, never stopping to think about what I meant by those important words. Back then, I was about as analytical as a squid.

So I told Nancy "I love you" without even giving it much thought. Or prayer. Looking back on it, I'm sure I did love Nancy. But I was still guilty of tossing those words around lightly.

We all toss words around lightly. But I wouldn't recommend misusing words of love. That doesn't mean you and your girl-friend have to write a fifty-page report on your feelings. It simply means you need to value your words. Know what you feel and say it. Communicate clearly.

And while you're at it, ask your doctor to check for any missing ribs.

GETTING *Really* SERIOUS

Love. We talked about it a little bit in the previous chapter on "Getting Serious." But just to make sure you get good and tired of the subject, we're going to talk about it a little more in this chapter on "Getting *Really* Serious."

At this stage of your relationship, you're probably beginning to ask yourself, "Am I in love? What is love? Does love last forever? Or does love only last as long as my acne medicine keeps working? Do people really 'fall' in love? Or do people 'step' in love? And if they step in love, can they ever get it off the bottom of their shoes?"

A lot of people like to divide love into different categories. In doing this, they usually refer to the three definitions created by the Greeks: *philia*, or friendship love; *eros*, or sexual love; and *agape*, or sacrificial, Godlike love.

Personally, I think they missed a few. Like these:

Amnesia love—This is the love that a mother has for her children, even though she can't ever get their names straight and says things like, "Bob, take out the—I mean Steve, take out the—I mean Wendy, take out the garbage! What do you mean you're just the paper boy? Well, whoever you are, take out the garbage!"

Brotherly love—This is incredibly powerful love. It has to be, because it can be awfully hard to love your older brother when he is sitting on your chest and threatening to drop worms on your face if you tell Mom that he exploded the potatoes in the microwave.

Sisterly love—Is this possible?

Second-cousin, twice-removed love—In the history of the world, only one person has ever experienced this kind of love because he's the only person who knows what a second cousin, twice removed is.

So how do you know if you are in love? Let me tell you. If your heart is racing, you're out of breath, and you're beginning to sweat, there is a 75 percent chance you are in love and a 25 percent chance you are being chased by a pit bull.

Which leads to the next question, "How do I express my love?" In some countries, hugging is a popular expression of love. In fact, in some countries even men go around hugging each other. In the United States, on the other hand, 95 percent of our hugging occurs when a contestant wins a pool table on "The Price Is Right."

So, as I said before, this chapter will deal with love. But it will also deal with many other touchy subjects that come up when two people get *really* serious. In other words, we're also going to talk a little bit about sex and marriage.

OFFICIAL
WRONG STUFF
GUIDE

*Falling in Love
and Acting Deranged*

Love and Phone Calls

1. Look at the clock and note that it's fifteen minutes to one o'clock. You told Mary you would call her at one o'clock.

2. Ask your parents if they would mind taking a walk around the block because you need some privacy.

3. Remind your parents to dress warmly because it's seventy-five degrees below zero outside and the snow is deep enough to bury Kareem Abdul Jabbar to his forehead.

4. Locate your stopwatch because your brother said that people in love talk on the phone for at least an hour at a time.

5. Locate your list of questions and answers that you wrote out ahead of time so you wouldn't have any awkward silences on the phone.

6. Call Mary.

7. When her mother answers, cringe when

you hear her whisper to someone, "It's that crazy boy who always drives over my rose bushes."

8. When Mary gets on the phone, ask her several of the questions on your list.

9. When she says, "Herman, it sounds like you're reading from something," flip to the answer that you wrote out just in case she said something like that.

10. Read your response, which goes like this: "Oh gee, does it sound like I ... (pause to flip the page) am reading something? Isn't that funny? Ha! Ha! Ha!"

11. When you run out of questions to ask Mary, check your stopwatch to find out if one hour has elapsed.

12. After you notice that only two minutes and 34.45 seconds have elapsed, shake the watch to make sure it's working.

13. Glance out the window and notice that your parents are burning the tires of their car to stay warm.

14. Suddenly realize that neither you nor Mary has said anything for the last ten seconds.

15. Panic.

16. Wonder what you should say.

17. Remember that your brother said that if you love someone, you should tell her so at least four times per week.

18. Wonder whether you should say, "I love you."

19. Try to get the courage to say, "I love you."

20. Begin to sweat because the silence is getting longer and the tension is building.

21. Notice that the stopwatch says one minute and 45.06 seconds have elapsed since the last time someone spoke.

22. Take a deep breath and say, "Mary, I love you."

23. Jump three feet when you hear the voice of Mary's mother say, "Mary's not here right now. She asked me to hold the phone while she went to the bathroom."

Love and Deep Conversations

1. Invite Mary over to your house after school.

2. When the two of you are sitting in your backyard and Mary asks if you could have a deep conversation, ask her, "Why?"

3. When she says deep conversations make people closer, agree to try it.

4. Attempt to listen closely when Mary tells you her views on war and peace, poverty, interstellar space travel, economic theories, racism, American history, the Bible, famous composers, and things at home that really get her down.

5. When she asks you to share something deep, tell her you were really bummed when the White Sox lost a three-game series to Oakland.

6. After Mary accepts the fact that you're shallow, ask if her mom mentioned anything about yesterday's phone call.

7. To be more specific, ask if her mom mentioned anything about what you said while she was holding the phone.

8. Cringe when Mary says, "My mom handed the phone back to me, and then she suddenly dropped to her knees and started praying that you would become a missionary to Africa ... very, very soon."

9. Say thank you when Mary hands you some literature that her mom gathered on how to become a missionary to Africa.

10. Decide it's time to try saying "I love you" again.

11. Try to get the courage to say "I love you."

12. Begin to sweat because you know she can tell you are nervous.

13. Begin to get more nervous because you know she can tell you are sweating.

14. Sweat some more because she can tell you are getting even more nervous.

15. Start to say, "I lo —"

16. Hear the phone ring.

17. Answer it.

18. When you hear the voice of Mary's mother on the other end of the line, tell her, "Yes, Mary remembered to give me the literature you collected on Africa."

19. Say, "Thank you for the material," and then hang up.

20. When you get back to Mary, find out she has to leave suddenly.

21. When Mary is gone, go upstairs and practice saying "I love you" to the hat rack.

Love and Marriage

1. Before driving to Mary's house, go up to your room and look in the mirror.

2. As you stare into the mirror, flatten your arms against your sides, making your biceps look bigger than they really are.

3. Check to see if you've been gaining any weight.

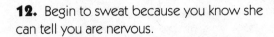

4. Wonder if it's your imagination when you notice you are starting to get "love handles"—the excess weight males get on their waist just above their hips.

5. Cringe when your brother peeks in and says, "They look more like 'love railings' to me."

6. Drive to Mary's house.

7. Before going up to the door of Mary's house, try to find out if you have bad breath: Breathe into your cupped hands and sniff. If you smell anything other than your hands, pop a breath mint.

8. Knock at Mary's door.

9. When Mary's mom answers the door, shake hands with the African missionary she invited over to talk with you.

10. After the missionary gives you a book on learning Swahili and demonstrates the tribal drums, say, "Nice to meet you" and go into the backyard where Mary is sitting.

11. To impress Mary, talk about deep things that matter to you, like the fact that the White Sox don't have a good left-hander to go against the Angels.

12. Wonder whether this would be a good time to tell Mary, "I love you."

13. Take a deep breath.

14. Wonder whether this is the moment to say, "I love you."

15. Start to say, "I lo —"

16. Feel total shock when Mary suddenly says, "What do you think about marriage?"

17. Feel an overwhelming sense of joy because you never knew she thought of you in terms of such commitment.

18. Try to sound very thoughtful and mature when you ask Mary, "Don't you think it's too soon to begin thinking about marriage?"

19. Become baffled when Mary says, "You may be right. After all, we just met this morning."

20. In a confused voice, say, "We met this morning?"

21. Sink into your chair when Mary says, "Yeah, I just met Donald this morning while playing tennis, but I'm afraid to tell Mom about him. Whenever guys start getting interested in me, she gives them literature on how to become missionaries in a foreign country. Which is why I got confused when she started giving you missionary literature. We're just best friends, but she must think we're getting serious. Isn't that funny?"

22. Pull out your list of questions and responses and read the words "Ha, ha, that's funny" from the sheet as you sink deeper in your chair.

23. Tell Mary you're not feeling very well.

24. Excuse yourself.

25. Start reading the book on Swahili and practicing the tribal drums.

26. Call up the African Missionary Board and ask if there are any openings.

27. Tell God, "I love you." He'll listen.

Clifford's Notes on The Scarlet Letter Sweater

The goal of the *Clifford's Notes* series is to summarize many of the greatest works of literature. So don't ask me how *The Scarlet Letter Sweater* ended up as part of our series.

The Scarlet Letter Sweater was written by Nathaniel Hee-Hawthorne, an incompetent eighteenth-century author who revolutionized writing by being the first to dot his *i*'s with smiley faces. With a contribution like that, Nathaniel obviously wasn't a terribly famous writer. Terribly famous writers are required to be depressed a lot (no smiley faces for them). Whenever terribly famous writers feel

good, they stay home, phone the office, and "call in well." Terribly famous writers get about thirty "well days" every year—days they stay home waiting to get depressed again.

No, Nathaniel Hee-Hawthorne is not a terribly famous writer. But his writing deserves at least a modicum of our attention. So let's turn to our *Clifford's Notes* summary of *The Scarlet Letter Sweater* and begin our analysis of this trivial piece of fluff.

CHAPTER 1
Summary

In chapter 1, the reader is introduced to the heroine, Hester Pringle, a high school cheerleader who has done the most awful thing. At Coldicut High School, hers is a crime of the first degree. It is outrageous. Unheard of! Extraordinary!

For her crime, Hester is forced to remove the school letter from her cheerleader's uniform. And in its place, she has to wear a blazing scarlet letter *A*.

What is her crime, you ask? Abstinence, of course. In this chapter, word gets around that Hester believes in abstaining from sex until marriage, and it has the school up in arms.

Her fellow students can't believe it. What's more, they're outraged that she's been attending movies containing explicit scenes of abstinence. Something has to be done. And quick!

So Hester is forced to stand in public every day for an hour, displaying her scarlet *A*.

Analysis

Nathaniel Hee-Hawthorne liked to use a lot of symbols in his books. His basement was probably crammed with old symbols that he didn't feel good about throwing away. So he got rid of them by putting them into his stories wherever possible. It was easier than holding a garage sale.

For example, the weeds at the beginning of this story symbolize corruption, the school cafeteria symbolizes indigestion, and the brief appearance of a Chicago Cubs player symbolizes losing.

CHAPTER 2
Summary
In this chapter, Nathaniel Hee-Hawthorne provides more detail on the setting for his story—Coldicut High School in eighteenth-century New England. This was a grim period of American history, a time when the Impuritans tried to impose their looser-than-thou attitude on others.

The Impuritans, as you probably know, came to America a little after the Puritans arrived at Plymouth Rock in the *Mayflower*.

The Impuritans traveled to America in the *Maycrabgrass*, a boat that tended to go around and around and around—maybe because the ship's captain used the type of compass that you draw circles with.

In this chapter, we also find out that somebody has a secret crush on Hester Pringle. But he's afraid to admit it.

Analysis
There is a bunch of words in this chapter.

CHAPTER 3
Summary
Aha! At this point in the story, you discover that the captain of the football team, Todd Dimwiddle, is the one with the crush on Hester Pringle. But he's terrified to admit it. If the guys find out that he wants to date a girl who believes in abstaining from sex until marriage, he'll lose his macho image.

While introducing us to Todd, the football captain, Nathaniel Hee-Hawthorne touches on the mysteries of male adolescence. Adolescence, he says, is that confusing time when many changes occur in a boy's body. For example, if your locker is next to the school bully, you may be getting more bruises on your face. The bruises will stimulate the development of facial hair, which is soon replaced by large quantities of tissue

paper where you cut yourself shaving. In fact, it may look like someone T.P.'d your face. And, of course, sweat glands develop during the teen years. You may sweat so much that your father suggests installing aluminum gutters along your arms.

As we learn in this chapter, Todd, the football captain, is experiencing dramatic changes such as these. And he's head-over-heels in love with Hester.

Analysis
Todd is obviously dominated by his hormones. Hormones are those little things in your bloodstream. They run around telling your body to do things, but they should not be confused with gym teachers.

CHAPTER 4
Summary
Stung by the rejection of her friends, Hester Pringle seeks help from the school guidance counselor. She asks whether it is really so bad to believe that sex is to be preserved for the lifelong commitment of marriage.

There is no right or wrong in life, the guidance counselor says (which is probably why everyone likes to take tests from him).

Todd is afraid because he faces rejection from both sides. He faces rejection from Hester if she says no. He also faces rejection from his Impuritan friends if she says yes, and they find out he's dating a girl who believes in abstinence.

Suddenly, Todd realizes something significant. Maybe Hester believes in sexual abstinence only because she has never had a guy suggest the alternative. What if a handsome hunk like him suggests they secretly spend the night together?

With his charm, Todd is sure he could convince Hester to forget her silly notion of abstaining until marriage.

This chapter ends with Todd bouncing the idea off the guidance counselor. "There is no right or wrong," the guidance counselor says. "It would not be right for me to tell you whether spending the night together is right or wrong. In addition, it would not even be right for me to say whether it would be right to ...".

Analysis

I'm beginning to wonder whether the guidance counselor should have stayed with his original profession—proofreading graffiti for a Los Angeles street gang.

CHAPTER 6
Summary

This chapter will stun you. Who would have thought Hester would say yes to Todd's suggestion that they spend the night together? But in this chapter, she does. She really does ... under one condition. Todd first must have a meal at Hester's favorite restaurant—a health food restaurant.

Not only that, but he has to eat the same food as Hester, and he has to eat it in exactly the way she suggests.

He tells Hester it would not be right for him to tell her whether premarital sex is right or wrong. In addition, he says it would not be right for him to say that it would not be right to tell her whether premarital sex is right or wrong. He says it would not even be right for him to say that it would not be right to say that it would not be right to tell her whether premarital sex is right or wrong. And it would not ...

Analysis

This is a long chapter.

CHAPTER 5
Summary

Todd, the football captain, is seriously tempted to phone Hester and ask her for a date. But he can't make himself do it.

YES, BUT...

McDARMA'S HEALTH FOOD MENU

JUST DO IT

Analysis

Nathaniel throws us for a loop in this chapter. I mean, why would Hester say yes? Even more confusing, why would Todd agree to eat at one of those health food restaurants with the foul-tasting meals? As the old saying goes, "Health food doesn't extend life, but it does make long life less desirable."

CHAPTER 7

Summary

In this dramatic scene, Hester and Todd steal away together. But as agreed, they first stop at the world famous health food establishment, where they serve tofu ten trillion different ways.

Hester orders her favorite, tofu á la brussels sprouts, while Todd begins to wonder whether this is just a dream. Is he really going to spend the night with Hester Pringle? Then he looks down at his tofu á la brussels sprouts and wonders whether he is really going to eat this stuff.

As Todd begins to chew his first bite, Hester matter-of-factly tells Todd to spit it out. At first, Todd just smiles at her rather strange joke.

"I'm not kidding, Todd. Spit it out."

"In public?"

"Yes, in public."

"But why spit out my food?"

"Because it tastes good," Hester says. She doesn't sound like she's joking. "I love the taste of this food," she adds. "That's why I like to keep spitting it out. And if you'll remember, you agreed to eat your food the way I suggest."

Todd notices they are attracting stares from a nearby table.

"If I might be nosey," he whispers, "you might tell me why you would spit out food you love."

"Because I love the *taste*. I figure that if I don't swallow the food, I'll have the appetite to go on tasting it all night long."

Todd is floored. "That's ridiculous!" he says. He's not only losing his appetite for this meal, but for the entire evening as well.

That, says Hester, is exactly her point. As C. S. Lewis once put it, separating sex from marriage is a lot like chewing food and spitting it out. Some people become so enthralled with the sensation of sex that they are willing to separate it from the emotional and spiritual commitment of marriage. It's like being so enthralled with the sensation of taste that you separate it from the process of swallowing and digestion. You chew your food for its taste, but then you spit it out.

"So go ahead," Hester says to Todd. "Spit out your food."

"What you ask is crazy!"

"I agree. And what you asked me to do is even crazier."

Smiling, Hester hands Todd some money to pay for the check. Then she leaves, brushing past their waiter. The waiter turns to look at her, then glances down at Hester's still full plate. "I assume the *A* on the young lady's sweater does not stand for 'appetite,'" he says.

Todd glances up at the waiter, still

stunned. Then his expression slowly remolds into a grin. "No," he smiles. "The *A* stands for 'amazing.'"

Analysis
   A also stands for "Amen."

Married in the Air

On their wedding day, many brides and grooms feel like they are floating on air. For Lou Szarka and Gloria E. Kearns, however, that feeling was real. They were married two thousand feet over the ground in a glider.

The ceremony was conducted by radio as the best man, maid of honor, and notary public soared nearby in their gliders.
   Source: *The 1989 Guinness Book of World Records,* New York: Sterling Publishing Co., 1988.

The Oldest Bridegroom

Harry Stevens of Wisconsin is the oldest bridegroom on record. In 1984, the 103-year-old Stevens married 84-year-old Thelma Lucas.
   Source: *The 1989 Guinness Book of World Records,* New York: Sterling Publishing Co., 1988.

Married in Kindergarten?

Records show many child marriages in England from 1561–66. For example, John Rigmarden (age three) married a bride who was five years old.
   Source: E. S. Turner, *A History of Courting,* New York: E. P. Dutton, 1955.

It's About Time!

In 1969, an 82-year-old woman and an 82-year-old man married in Mexico City. They had been engaged for sixty-seven years.
   Source: Stephen Pile, *The Incomplete Book of Failures,* New York: E. P. Dutton, 1979.

Back-Walking Brides

On the Cook Islands in the Pacific Ocean, brides used to be given a unique version of the "red carpet" treatment. All the men in the

village would lie down on their bellies, and the bride would walk on their backs all the way from her house to her new husband's house.

Source: A. Hyatt Verrill, *Strange Customs, Manners, and Beliefs,* Boston: L. C. Page and Company, 1946.

What's a Best Man?

There are several theories of how we came up with the tradition of best man, groomsmen, and bridesmaids at weddings.

Some people believe the idea of "best man" refers to a time when men captured their brides by force. To steal away a woman, the groom brought along the best fighters he could find—his best men.

Another theory claims that groomsmen and bridesmaids were used to fool evil spirits. People believed that evil spirits could cause trouble during a wedding service. Therefore, to confuse the spirits, groomsmen and bridesmaids dressed up like the bride and groom and went down the aisle first.

Source: Tad Tuleja, *Curious Customs,* New York: Harmony Books, 1987.

I Now Pronounce You "Rock and Wife"

In 1976, before a crowd of twenty people, a Los Angeles woman married a

fifty-pound rock.

Source: David Louis, *More Fascinating Facts,* New York: Crown Publishers, 1979.

Get Engaged or Get Dunked

At one time on the island of Borkum, it wasn't wise for a man to keep dating a woman without ever setting a wedding date.

Evidently, other males in the village would surround the man's house and block the chimney, filling the place with smoke. Then they would climb in through the roof and ask the man, "Are you engaged?" If the man said yes, they would celebrate. But if the man said no, they would tie a rope to him and drag him through a pond three times.

Source: *Strange Stories, Amazing Facts,* Pleasantville, New York: The Reader's Digest Association, 1976.

I Now Pronounce You "Husband and Tree"

The Brahmans in southern India have a law that says a younger brother cannot marry until after the older brother marries. However, if the older brother is having trouble finding a wife, there is a way around the rule. The older brother can be married to a tree.

Source: William J. Fielding, *Strange Customs of Courtship and Marriage,* reprint of 1942 edition, Darby, Pennsylvania: Darby Books, 1980.

Were Ancient Greeks Really That Smart?

Ancient Greeks may have been advanced in many ways. But their treatment of females was not one of them.

A Greek girl was confined to the house

almost the entire period from birth to marriage. Only on her wedding day would the woman be the center of attention as she paraded through the streets to the music of flutes. But after the wedding day, wives spent most of their remaining years back in the house. Rarely, if ever, were they seen in the streets.

Source: Morton M. Hunt, *The Natural History of Love*, New York: Alfred A. Knopf, 1959.

Marriage by Bottle

As a British sailor was about to leave for India sometime in the nineteenth century, he

wrote out a marriage proposal, placed it in a bottle, and tossed the bottle into the ocean. I'm not sure how he expected to find himself a wife with such a strategy. But he did it anyway and sailed to India.

Later, when the sailor was about to board a ship bound from India back to England, he spotted a bottle floating toward shore. Plucking the bottle from the water, he opened it. Inside was his very own marriage proposal.

Source: David Wallechinsky, Irving Wallace, and Amy Wallace, *The Book of Lists*, New York: William Morrow and Company, 1977.

Equal-Opportunity Harems

In ancient days, men weren't the only ones to have harems. Queen Kahena of Aurès, Algeria, had four hundred men in her harem.

Source: Kevin McFarland, *Incredible!*, Hart Publishing Company, 1976.

The Four Mistakes

In the words of Brian, business management consultant:

I had been dating a girl for about seven months when her sixteenth birthday approached. I was eighteen at the time, and I wanted to take her out some place special for her birthday. So I found out about a romantic Italian restaurant in downtown Chicago. (I lived in the suburbs.)

I had about fifty-two dollars, and we drove downtown thinking we were going to have a great time. But it wasn't long before we ran into mistake number one. I couldn't find the restaurant. I had never been to this restaurant before, and I didn't know the city very well, so we looked and looked and looked. I didn't even have the restaurant's phone number to call. Needless to say, I felt more nervous and stupid every passing minute.

Finally, we realized we had missed our reservations. .That's when I remembered that a friend had told me about another place— the ninety-fifth floor of the John Hancock Building. So I thought, "Why not? Let's go for it."

After making reservations for nine o'clock, we went over to the planetarium by the lake to talk. I forgot about my worries, thinking that the ninety-fifth floor of the John Hancock would be even better than the Italian restaurant.

It was better, all right. More than better—luxurious, opulent, *expensive*. I could tell it was expensive when my date looked at her menu and said, "This is strange. I don't have any prices on my menu."

My menu had prices, though, and I saw they were extremely high for the minimal amount of money I had in my pocket. Mistake number two of the evening. But I told myself I was going to make the best of it and act really cool, as if it didn't bother me.

We ordered filet mignon for two, but I told her we had to be careful about ordering much else. So we got filet mignon for two, with some vegetables and water. The waiters, all in tuxedos, were top-notch. They even cleaned off our table with a whisk broom. When they brought a dessert tray, I panicked because the desserts were really expensive, so I told my date, "Let's not have dessert tonight."

I asked if she had any money, noting that I didn't have a lot myself, but she said no. So we got the bill, and I became very nervous.

The bill ended up being forty-eight dollars. I had enough money, but I thought, "What am I going to do? I don't have money for a tip!"

I knew that in this kind of restaurant, you normally overpay and then don't ask for any change. But tonight I paid the bill exactly, right down to the change. Then I decided to roll up three dollars in my hand. I walked over to the waiter and shook his hand with the money in my palm, slipping him the money as I said, "Excellent service, sir, excellent!" He smiled, stuck his hand in his pocket and said, "Thank you, sir, thank you." My plan worked. When he said, "Thank you," he didn't even look to find out how much money I was slipping him. For all he knew, the little roll of three dollars I gave could have been one hundred dollars. Three dollars for a fifty-dollar meal is pretty cheap. It's called "getting stiffed."

We went to the coat check place; and all of a sudden, I realized everybody was paying the coat-check girl for their coats. I was shocked, so we just stood and watched people for about five minutes to see how this was done. When we realized that some people didn't pay, we followed suit, got our coats, and left.

Then came mistake number three. I thought, "I've only got a dollar left. I hope the garage where we parked the car isn't going to be a problem." It was about midnight when we got the car from the parking garage and pulled it up to the cashier's booth. I said, "How much?" And he said, "Four bucks."

"But I've only got a dollar," I said.

And he said, "Sorry."

"But I've only got a dollar. I'm a young kid and don't have much money."

"We're sorry. We can't let you out," he said.

keys in the car.

When I paid the garage attendant his four dollars, he changed into Mr. Nice Guy, got out a hanger, and got our car open.

Everything seemed to go wrong that night. But at least I treated my girlfriend to a memorable sweet sixteen!

The Nose and the Kiss

In the words of Stephen R. Melton, associate pastor

When I was in high school, there was one girl I really wanted to date. Her name was Ava. She was beautiful. I was entranced by her long brown hair and sparkling blue eyes. It took me months to get up the courage to ask her out. When she said yes, I couldn't believe it.

I was only fifteen, so we had to ride the fan bus to the basketball game. The entire evening I had one thing on my mind: "If I could only kiss Ava!"

On the ride home, we sat in the back. Every time she smiled or squeezed my hand, I nearly fainted. I knew I had to make my move now—we were almost home. As I turned toward Ava, my heart was pounding. My ears were hot. I leaned over to kiss her and then it happened. My nose started to bleed. I mean, *it bled.*

When I was young, my nose had been broken, so the vessels were weak. Whenever I got too excited or my blood pressure got too high, it would bleed.

There was blood on Ava's sweater and my white pants, and it didn't take long for the whole bus (and school) to hear what happened. No kiss that night. A disastrous date.

Fortunately, Ava didn't hold it against me. After my nose and I got a little older, Ava and I got married.

We got out of the car and decided to pray about this mess. There had to be something we could do. We went up to a doorman, and he looked at us strangely. He didn't say a word to us when we tried to ask for money. He didn't even answer us.

All of a sudden, we spotted a limousine. Two chauffeurs leaned against it, talking. We explained the whole story to one of the chauffeurs, and he thought it was the funniest thing. He just laughed, pulled out a wad of money and said, "How much do you need?" Then, after paying us, he said, "Instead of paying me back, just give it to the church."

So we got to the car, all excited, and I pulled the door handle. It was locked. I said to my date, "Did you take the keys?"

Mistake number four. I had locked the

Revenge of the Macaroni and Cheese Dinner

In the words of Barry Kilmer, associate pastor:

On my second date with a girl I liked very much, I thought I would impress her with a little trick. The Christian college we both attended was famous for their thick macaroni and cheese. The consistency was so firm that you could turn the plate upside down and the macaroni wouldn't budge.

When I attempted this feat on our date, however, the macaroni and cheese must not have been mixed to the same consistency. For when I turned the plate over, there was approximately a three-second delay before the entire helping dropped into my lap.

The episode impressed my date so much that she ended up marrying me two years later.

The Man Who Made a Big Mistake

In some cultures of the past, capturing women was an all-too-common way that men obtained mates. Even in recent decades, this revolting practice has been used. But fortunately, it is not always successful.

In 1972, a man in Damali (on the Black Sea) decided to abduct a woman who wouldn't show any interest in him. He threw a blanket over the woman in the middle of the night and carried her away, all the while murmuring words of love. In the morning he unwrapped the woman from the blanket, only to discover he had mistakenly taken the woman's 91-year-old grandmother. The old woman promptly gave him a deserved beating.

Source: Stephen Pile, *The Incomplete Book of Failures*, New York: E. P. Dutton, 1979.

The Clumsy Man

One weekend in the late 1800s, a London teacher was visiting the family of the woman he intended to ask to marry. Unfortunately, while getting a drink of water in the middle of the night, he accidentally knocked ink all over the family's priceless tapestry. Mortified, he fled.

THE DATING HALL OF SHAME

After allowing some time to pass, the man made another attempt to propose marriage. Figuring that nothing could go wrong in half an hour, he arranged for a meeting with the woman. But when he moved to sit on what he thought was a cushion, he accidentally sat on the family's small but precious dog, killing it.

The man left immediately. He never proposed.

Source: Stephen Pile, *The Incomplete Book of Failures*, New York: E. P. Dutton, 1979.

The Man Who Married the Wrong Person

Jacob grew up to be a great man of God, an Old Testament founding father. But in his younger years, he could be downright crafty.

Jacob tricked his brother, Esau, into giving him his birthright. And he tricked his father into giving him a special blessing—a blessing intended for the oldest son, Esau. I wouldn't be surprised if Jacob were the type of brother to steal girlfriends from Esau. You know the type I mean: the kind who can't even look at someone else's girl without wanting her for his own.

Jacob eventually got a taste of his own medicine in an incident deserving of the Dating Hall of Shame. He met a girl named Rachel by the well (the Old Testament equivalent of meeting at the mall). Being a bold fellow, Jacob gave Rachel a big kiss, and he was so overjoyed, he began to weep. Either that, or she bit him in the lip by mistake.

Without hesitation, Jacob asked Rachel's father, Laban, if he could marry Rachel. "Sure," Laban said. "But you have to put in seven years of work for me first."

Talk about a tough way to get a date. But Jacob agreed to the seven years of work

anyway. His job was to watch over the flock, which is where they got their food back then since they didn't have fast-food restaurants. I guess you could say that Laban's demand would be like a father today asking you to work for him at Burger Heaven for seven years before you could marry his daughter. (The main difference is that shepherds went around in animals' skins, which were a lot more stylish than fast-food uniforms.)

After Jacob had put in seven years of work, his wedding day finally arrived. There was only one problem. A bride back then was covered in so many veils that you couldn't see her face. That's why Jacob had no idea that Laban had put his older daugh-

ter, Leah, in Rachel's place. Without knowing it, Jacob married Leah instead of Rachel.

When Jacob later confronted Laban about the trick, Laban probably responded with the Hebrew word for "Oops." Then he told Jacob it was their custom for the older sister to get married first. "But I tell you what," he said. "If you agree to put in another seven years of work, I'll let you marry Rachel at the end of this week. Then you can have two wives!"

Such a deal. So Jacob agreed to another seven years at Burger Heaven. If Jacob's older brother, Esau, had heard about Laban's trick, he probably would have laughed till he cried.

Source: *Holy Bible: The New International Version*, the book of Genesis, chapter 29, Grand Rapids: Zondervan Bible Publishers.

Playfood

C. S. Lewis liked to use food to illustrate points about sex outside of marriage. You saw one example in the story, *The Scarlet Letter Sweater*. Now I'm going to give you another example.

Imagine you're in a land where people are obsessed with food. A land where the most popular magazine is *Playfood*, complete with centerfold photos of food. A land with adult food stores, where people peer through peepholes in refrigerators and drool over the food inside. A land where people gather in

large audiences to watch someone on stage uncover a large casserole, while provocative music plays. A land where moviemakers think that every film has to include a scene of people eating dinner because they know it's going to get a lot of people excited.

As Lewis points out in *Mere Christianity* (New York, Macmillan, 1964), if you stumbled across a country like that, wouldn't you think something had gone wrong with its desire for food? By the same token, if aliens from another planet landed on earth, wouldn't they think something had gone wrong with our sexual desires?

Sexual feelings are natural and healthy. That's why it is sad to see these feelings twisted, mass-produced, packaged, and exploited in our culture.

Back to the Dark Ages

In twelfth-century France, some people had the wacky notion that love and romance could *not* be found in marriage. Marriage was for raising families, not for romance.

As an example, historians cite a case in which a woman loved a man. I don't know the woman's name, but for the sake of this story, we'll call her Jenny. When Jenny made her feelings known, she discovered that the man loved another woman, whom we'll call Abigail. However, the man promised that if he ever stopped loving Abigail, he would give his love to Jenny.

Well, as it turned out, the man didn't stop loving Abigail. In fact, he ended up marrying her. But because many people actually believed love couldn't exist within a marriage, Jenny claimed that the man could no longer love Abigail. Therefore, he had to give his love to her instead, as promised.

Jenny even went as far as to take the case before the "court of love," which decided matters of the heart. The court decided that, yes, the man had to give his love to Jenny, even though he was married to Abigail.

The strange thing is, the philosophy we get from movies and television today is strikingly similar to this bizarre belief from twelfth-century France. Movies and TV bombard us with the notion that romance and love can only be found *outside* of marriage. They glorify premarital sex and extramarital affairs. In his book, *Lost in the Cosmos*, Walker Percy reports that only 6 percent of the sexual encounters presented on soap operas are between a husband and wife.

We've gone back to the Dark Ages. Will someone please turn on the lights?

CHAPTER 5

THE FIGHT OF THE CENTURY

Psychologists at the University of Washington conducted an experiment that, at first glance, may seem to have nothing to do with dating. But only at first glance.

According to John Nicholson's book, *Habits*, people in this experiment were shown film clips of a traffic accident. Then they were asked to estimate the speed of the cars in the accident. The interesting thing is that when people were asked, "How fast were the cars going when they *contacted* each other?" most of them named a speed below thirty-two miles per hour. But when people were asked, "How fast were the cars going when they *smashed into* each other?" most of

them gave speeds closer to forty miles per hour.

As you can see, the use of different words affected the way people remembered the accident. When researchers used the stronger words *"smashed into,"* people tended to think that the cars were traveling faster.

The researchers did a similar experiment with another group of people, only this time they asked whether the viewers saw any shattered glass in the accident. Once again, the use of different words affected their memories. When the researchers used strong words, such as *"smashed into,"* many more people said they remembered seeing smashed glass ... even though no glass had been smashed at all.

These experiments tell me a couple of things. First, they tell me that our memories can be awfully flawed. Yet we often let these flawed memories create major conflicts with our girlfriends and boyfriends. "I know you said those mean things to me last week and I was really teed off!" you shout. Then your boyfriend yells back, "You're crazy! I never said anything of the kind!"

The second thing these experiments tell me is that emotionally loaded words can alter our memories. When we keep telling ourselves, "She screamed at me" or "He acted like a total idiot" or "He was absolutely and completely unreasonable," these emotionally loaded words may actually alter the way we remember a conflict. Even if your girlfriend spoke in only a slightly irritated voice, you may convince yourself that she yelled at you.

People say some pretty wild things in the heat of a fight. People also *do* some pretty wild things. Ann Landers, the advice columnist, once told of a man who had a political disagreement with his wife, so he hid her

dentures to prevent her from going out in public and voting for a candidate he didn't like. Talk about a heavy-handed use of power.

To get some lessons on how to act really

weird in the midst of dating conflicts, we turn to this chapter—"The Fight of the Century." Along with another step-by-step guide to the Wrong Stuff, we will visit the world of hobbits and examine the use of power in relationships. And if in the end you don't like the chapter, we can step out back and have it out.

Going Unsteady

The Girl's Perspective

1. When you see your boyfriend, Larry, in the school hallway, ask him if he studied hard last night for the history test.

2. When he changes the subject and starts talking about the insects he studied in biology class, notice that his shirt smells like perfume.

3. Ask Larry why his shirt smells like a brand of perfume that you never wear.

4. When Larry keeps talking about a type of ant that will self-explode to send a warning signal to other ants, tell him *you're* going to explode if you don't get an explanation about the perfume.

5. Try to listen patiently when he says he was sitting next to Flora Barnes in biology class, and she wears so much perfume that a million perfume molecules must have attached to his shirt by just being in the same room with her.

6. Start to lose patience when he rambles on about how Flora probably applies perfume with a garden hose, and how she wears so much blush on her face that it looks like her cheeks were hit by hockey pucks.

7. Notice that Larry has some blond hairs on his shirt collar. Get suspicious because Larry has a black flattop.

8. Get even more suspicious when he says that while he was looking for a hat in the closet this morning, his mom's wig collection fell on him, and some

blond hairs must have gotten on his shirt.

9. Really lose your cool when Larry pulls out a self-help book and reads a section that says, "Remind your partner that jealousy is caused by his or her insecurity, not your unfaithfulness. This needs to be repeated over and over again."

10. Ask him if that sentence bears repeating even if you're stuffing him in the school trash compactor.

11. Wonder if Larry is being honest when he goes on and on about how he would never look at another girl because he adores you.

12. When Larry says he puts you on a pedestal, remind him that he does the same thing to his stuffed moose head.

13. Stare in shock when Cindy Yoko walks by and tells Larry she had a good time last night.

14. Try to control yourself when Larry begins to stammer an explanation for "last night."

15. Try extra-hard to control yourself when Larry says he had been planning to study for the history test last night, but Eric called and asked if he'd like to go bowling. It just so happened that Eric had also asked a couple of girls to join them, which Larry says he really, really didn't know about.

16. Decide not to control yourself any longer.

17. Remove the ring from your finger and throw it at Larry.

18. Feel your anger rise when Larry picks up the ring, looks at it, and says, "I never gave you a ring."

19. Shout, "Of course not! You're too cheap, so I went out and bought a ring myself to throw in your face."

20. Tell Larry you never want to see him again.

21. Tell Larry you've hated his cheapness ever since you found out that his idea of "going out to eat" is to stand around in the grocery store, waiting for them to put out free samples.

22. Begin to sob.

23. As tears come down your face, blow your nose.

24. Feel like screaming when Larry pulls out his biology book and starts reading aloud. He's reading about how some of your tears are draining into the lacrimal glands in the corners of each eye. Then the fluid runs into your nasal ducts and down into your nose. That's why you have a runny nose.

25. Before running into the girl's rest room to sob, grab one of the blond hairs from Larry's shoulder so you can analyze it in chemistry class.

The Boy's Perspective

1. Walk to Julie's house after school and ask her if you could talk about your fight this morning.

2. Tell her you'll do anything to make things better.

3. Ask her what she wants you to do to make things better.

4. Ask her to define the word *grovel.*

5. Cringe when Julie asks you to apologize.

6. Tell her, "Love means never having to say you're sorry."

7. When she threatens you with a judo flip, tell her, "But fear often finds it is very necessary to say you're sorry."

8. Tell Julie you're sorry you went bowling with Eric, Cindy, and Lisa last night.

9. When Julie begins to calm down, take a walk to the park.

10. Tell Julie the only reason you went bowling with another girl last night was because you wanted "to find some space."

11. Tell Julie she should "own her own feelings."

12. Tell Julie "I'm OK, you're OK."

13. Tell Julie you'd like her to "share where she's coming from."

14. Tell Julie that "if she lives on the growing edge, she can become self-actualized."

15. Tell Julie you'll agree to stop reading from your goofy self-help book, but only if she gives it back to you and stops ripping pages out of it.

16. Put your self-help book in your backpack, take Julie's hand, and walk along in silence.

17. Tell her you're sorry again.

18. Put your arm around Julie and sit on a bench. Snuggle.

19. Panic when she smiles and playfully says, "I'll take the ring back and start wearing it again."

20. Try to change the subject by pulling out a book on insects and telling Julie how you learned this morning that termites build air-conditioned skyscrapers out of mud.

21. When Julie says she would really like to wear the ring again because she's feeling better about the relationship, start to stammer.

22. Decide that you can't lie.

23. In a stuttering voice, tell her you sold the ring to someone during the lunch hour.

24. When Julie explodes, tell her, "You said you didn't want the ring, and you threw it at me, and I didn't want to just leave it there on the ground where someone would take it."

25. Tell her you'll split the money with her.

26. Say, "OK, OK, I'll give you *all* the money, but could I have a 15 percent commission for selling the ring?"

27. Later, in the doctor's office, shake your head and sigh when Dr. Brady asks you how an eraser got jammed up your nose.

The Girl's Perspective

1. After Larry has left for the doctor's office with your eraser up his nose, notice that he left his book on insects sitting on the bench.

2. Open the book and read about how the black widow spider devours her husband for dinner.

3. Decide that the male spider probably deserved it.

The Lord of the Ring

Thick, dark clouds gathered on the horizon. There was tension in the air. As the news spread among the clouds—"Hey, there's a big hunk of tension in the air!"—all the clouds scurried over, climbing on top of each other to get a good look. Soon the storm clouds loomed threateningly high over the earth.

Our hero, a hobbit named Dodo, stared up at the gathering clouds and mumbled something deep and mysterious under his breath, about three inches under his breath, to be exact. Meanwhile, his courageous, loyal friend, a hobbit by the name of Spam Gamgee, put a hand on his sword, sensing danger.

Spam knew that the Nine Bicycle Riders were looking for *the ring*—the powerful ring that Dodo carried in his pocket. Spam also knew that the Nine Bicycle Riders would do *anything* to get their hands on it. They were dark, evil creatures, who traced people down and harassed them with untiring persistence. In our world, we call them lawyers.

People were fascinated with the ring because anyone who wore the all-powerful ring would instantly have complete control over members of the opposite sex. By slipping on the ring, even the most despised boy would suddenly find himself swarmed by cheerleaders and homecoming queens, all wanting to date him.

There was deep power in the ring. That is why Dodo knew he had to destroy it. He and Spam had a clear but deadly mission: They must take the ring to the top of Mt. Doom-de-doom-doom and cast it into the fire before the Nine Bicycle Riders could get their hands

Dodo knew there would never be peace between the sexes if the ring existed. He knew that whenever girls or guys try to hold power over one another, the result is nothing but pain and suffering.

A long time ago, in the misty past of Middle-Earth, peace had reigned between the sexes, for they had not had the weapons to fight each other. Back in the ancient Age of the Do-It-Yourselfers, all of the weapons had been assembled using the type of directions that accompany assemble-it-yourself lawn furniture—directions so useless that the instructions in sixteen other languages make more sense than the instructions in English.

Because of this problem, girls and guys had been unable to assemble their weapons, and the world had prospered.

But that was a long, long time ago. Now girls and guys were heavily armed with bows and arrows and swords and axes. Now they had something to fight over—the ring.

Suddenly, as Dodo and Spam reached the foot of Mt. Doom-de-doom-doom, they were besieged by the most deadly, most horrifying creatures that roamed Middle-Earth. No, they were not attacked by goblins. And not by orcs. They weren't even attacked by wolves or dragons.

Surrounding them, yipping, yapping, hopping, growling, was a pack of Mexican Chihuahuas, miniature poodles, and other small, obnoxious dogs. They jumped and panted, whined and worried, their little dog voices so high and piercing and persistent that Dodo and Spam thought they'd go insane from the noise.

Dodo stumbled to the rocky ground, cramming his hands into his ears to block the deadly sound. When he looked up, all he saw were little dog mouths, pink and black and gaping, and little dog bodies, hopping about like Mexican jumping beans.

Spam pulled at Dodo. "Get up, get up!" he cried. "We can't stay here!" But as he yanked at Dodo's arm, the world started to spin before his eyes. The barking increased.

Spam grew dizzier and dizzier. The noise filled his mind, his eyes, his nostrils, until he forgot there was such a thing as quiet, or any other noise but barking.

Just when Dodo and Spam thought they would die under the onslaught of noise, the barking stopped.

Quiet.

Dodo took several long, deep breaths before he mustered the energy to sit up and find out if he was dead or alive. He shook his head, rubbed his eyes, and looked around.

There stood Golly. Once a handsome hobbit who had charmed girls even without the ring, Golly had fallen in love with a girl who refused to love him. In desperation, he had turned to the power of the ring. But the ring had corrupted him. Golly's pleasant hobbit face had turned reptilian. His hard-working hobbit hands had narrowed, had become clutching and grasping. And now, his blackened scales dripping with slime, his eyes fixed and gleaming straight at Dodo, he cackled as he moved slowly toward Dodo.

"My precious," said Golly, extending his long, slippery hand. "Hand over my precious. Hand over the ring."

"Never," said Dodo. "The ring will destroy you even more than it has already."

"Hand over my precious, my ring, or I will tell the dogs to start barking again," Golly said, smiling, rubbing his hands together and snickering. (The American Association of Slimy Villains

requires all evil people to rub their hands together and snicker. Cackling is also accepted.)

"The ring will give you too much power over girls," Spam said, keeping a wary eye on the pack of Chihuahuas and miniature poodles.

"And what is wrong with having power over girls?"

"There's too much power-grabbing in relationships already," said Dodo. "Guys and girls are always trying to get the other person to love them the most. That way, if you can get a girl to flip out over you more than you're flipped out over her, then you can control her. She'll do anything you want just to keep you."

"He's right," Spam added. "I once loved a girl much more than she loved me. And she took advantage of her power. She treated me like dirt."

"Is that why she always dumped bags of fertilizer on you?" Dodo asked.

Spam nodded.

"I'll treat you worse than dirt if you don't hand over that ring," Golly said. The dogs were beginning to get edgy. Their whining sounded like an approaching swarm of mosquitoes.

"Now why don't you just settle down, Golly, and let us continue on our way," Dodo said, slowly beginning to move backwards.

"That's right," Spam said, following Dodo's lead. "You don't need this ring."

By this time, Spam and Dodo had moved about ten feet away from Golly, taking one slow step at a time. Golly seemed to be thinking about what they had said—you could almost see his mind moving in slow circles as he stood there, staring.

Then his face solidified into a scowl, and he turned to the dogs. "Get them!" he shouted.

As the dogs came alive, Dodo and Spam leaped into action. They scrambled up the side of Mt. Doom-de-doom-doom, the dogs hot on their trail.

At first, Dodo felt a surge of energy, and he very nearly flew up the side of the mountain, ignoring the dogs' constant barking. But then he began to weaken. A clamp seemed to squeeze the sides of his skull. The pain grew so intense that he tripped head over heels into a clump of bushes.

His head spinning, he looked up the side of Mt. Doom-de-doom-doom and realized he would never make it. The dogs were all over him. When he looked up, he saw at least twenty dogs right over his face going, "Yip, yip, yip, yip!"

There was only one thing left to do. Slowly his hand moved to his pocket, and he groped for the ring inside. Just then his vision doubled, tripled. Instead of twenty dogs, there were forty; instead of forty, sixty. The images overlapped and filled his entire field of vision, shuffling in and about, spinning and merging together in a kaleidoscope of Chihuahuas and poodles and dachshunds.

"Here is the ring," Dodo croaked, pulling it out of his pocket. "Golly, here is—"

But before Dodo could say anything else, and before he could hand the ring to Golly, the dogs had disappeared, running down the mountainside, their yipping growing more and more faint.

Slowly, Dodo pulled himself upright and looked over the edge of the mountain. There he saw a string of bicycles. The Nine Bicycle Riders! They had tracked him down, desperate for the ring. But right now they were surrounded by the pack of dogs, who found chasing bicycles infinitely more interesting than chasing Dodo and Spam.

"Dodo!" Spam called. He pulled Dodo from the bushes. "This is our chance to escape!"

But by now Golly was right behind the two fleeing hobbits, begging for the ring all the way. Spam and Dodo scrambled for the top of Mt. Doom-de-doom-doom. Dodo was three feet from the top when Golly grabbed his leg and pulled him down. The ring dropped from his hand and went skipping and twirling across a slab of rock.

Smoothly jumping over the fallen Dodo, Golly scooped up the ring. He waved it above his head and danced with delight.

"It's mine!" he shouted. "It's mine!" Then he put on the ring and smiled the most awful smile Dodo had ever seen. Golly knew that he now had power. He knew that this ring

was even more powerful than the old "if-I-paid-for-the-date-then-you-owe-me-something-in-return" power play that guys pull on girls. With this ring, all females everywhere would do his bidding. With this ring ...

As Golly continued to dance and cackle, something dark and horrible emerged from a nearby cave. Dodo and Spam gasped. There loomed a hairy spider the size of a huge boulder. At first, the monstrous spider seemed bent on attacking Dodo and Spam. But then it stopped and stared at Golly, who was too busy caressing his ring to notice.

It might have been Dodo's imagination, but he thought the spider sighed and smiled at Golly with the goony look his sister had whenever she flipped out over a rock star.

Yes, that *had* to be it. The spider was female, and because of the ring, she had fallen in love with Golly!

The spider crawled closer and closer. When she was just about to wrap her hairy legs around the poor slimy Golly, he came to. "Aauugh!" he screamed. He took off like a flash. Dodo and Spam watched him scamper across the rocks, the love-stricken spider in full pursuit.

"I didn't know Golly could run so fast," Spam said.

"Oh, but he's had lots of practice," Dodo said.

He was right about that. Power-hungry people get lots of practice running away from things.

The War of the Whiskers

Boyfriends and girlfriends can have some devastating fights. But fortunately, most of them don't result in outright war. That wasn't the case, however, with a fight that occurred in France during the twelfth century. It all started from something very silly—Lady Eleanor of France didn't like it when her husband returned from the Crusades in 1152 minus his beard.

When the king refused to grow his beard back, the queen divorced him and married the King of England. Then, when Lady Eleanor tried to convince two French provinces to switch their loyalty to her new English husband, a war erupted between England and France. Its name: the War of the Whiskers.

The war lasted three hundred years. And it all started with a beard. Or the lack of one.

Source: Stan Lee, *The Best of the Worst*, New York: Harper & Row, 1979.

Hand-in-Pipe

I have no idea if the following incident caused a lover's quarrel between Sir Isaac Newton and his lady friend, but it certainly had the potential.

Newton, the man who discovered gravity, was innocently walking hand-in-hand with a lady. But he must have had his mind on science, because Newton suddenly used his lady's finger to push down the tobacco in his pipe.

Source: E. S. Turner, *A History of Courting*, New York: E. P. Dutton, 1955.

Fair Fighting?

In medieval times, a husband and wife sometimes were allowed to settle disputes by fighting in front of a court. To make the battle more even, the man stood in a hole while his wife stood on level ground. Then they went at each other with clubs. The winner of the fight was declared victor in the dispute.

Source: William J. Fielding, *Strange Customs of Courtship and Marriage*, reprint of 1942 edition, Darby, Pennsylvania: Darby Books, 1980.

It's in the Bag

The world has never seen a duel like this one between a German and a Spaniard. They were both fighting for the right to marry Helene Acharfequinn.

Helene's father did not want to see the men spill blood by dueling with swords or pistols. So he said that whichever man could put the other one in a gunnysack could marry his daughter. After fighting for over an hour, Baron von Talbert (the German) finally stuffed his rival into a sack. Then he carried the sack over his shoulder, dropped it at Helene's feet, and asked if she would marry him.

Source: Bruce Felton and Mark Fowler, *Felton and Fowler's Best, Worst, and Most Unusual,* New York: Thomas Y. Crowell Company, 1975.

The Fan

At one time, the fan was a useful courting device, used to express emotions and convey romantic intentions.

You could use a fan to hit a man over the head, to hide blushes, or to drop when you wanted to catch a man's attention. To show anger, you'd snap your fan shut with a vicious clack.

There were also many languages of the fan. In one system, for example, touching the left cheek with the fan meant, "I want to get rid of you."

Source: E. S. Turner, A History of Courting , New York: E. P. Dutton, 1955.

Kissing Goes to Court

In 1837, an Englishman sued a girl because she bit him in the nose when he kissed her against her will. As it turned out, though, she won the case. According to the judge, "When a man kisses a woman against her will, she is fully entitled to bite his nose, if she so pleases."

Source: Robert Ebisch, "Paying Lip Service to That Historic Romantic—The Kiss," *Chicago Tribune,* 14 February 1986.

When Politeness Became Ridiculous

I'm all for politeness on dates, but there are limits. In eighteenth-century England, some men went to strange lengths to impress each other and their ladies with their politeness. Sometimes they even fought over who could be more polite.

For example, there was the time when the Duc de Coislin decided to politely escort his guest to a carriage. But the guest insisted on politely escorting Coislin back to his house. Not to be outdone, Coislin escorted the guest back to the carriage. But the guest turned right around and escorted Coislin back to his house. Not only that, the guest locked him in the house. However, a very determined Coislin then leaped out of a window so he could escort his guest back to the carriage.

After spraining his finger during the leap, Coislin went to the doctor. But he hurt the finger again when he and the doctor struggled over who could be the first to open the door politely for the other person.

Source: Morton M. Hunt, *The Natural History of Love,* New York: Alfred A. Knopf, 1959.

Family Ties

Watch what kind of present you give to your date, or you could get yourself into a major fight. In Poland in 1979, a man was fined because he forced his wife to *eat* an obnoxiously loud tie she had given him as a gift.

Source: Bill Bryson, Jr., *The Book of Bunders*, New York: A Dell/Jonathan David Book, 1982.

Not-So-Easy Rider

In the words of Jane Sutton, stay-at-home mother:

It seemed like an ordinary evening. Not in my wildest imagination could I have predicted the events to follow.

I had a date that evening with Dave, a quiet fellow from a much different crowd than I was used to. Nevertheless, I looked forward to going out with him and was delighted when he pulled up in my driveway on a motorcycle. We went to a party—I can't remember where—but I'll never forget the trip home.

After Dave sailed through a yellow light, I heard a siren and looked back to see red flashing lights. A police car was signaling us, and I fully expected Dave to pull over. Instead, he gunned it.

"Let me off!" I screamed.

"Hold on!" he yelled back.

So I held on desperately while we zigzagged through my subdivision, then zoomed over onto the highway. Everything passed in a blur. When I tried to look up, the wind knocked tears out of my eyes. Now there were two police cars screaming behind us, and up ahead I saw a roadblock. Dave would have to stop.

But he didn't. Unbelievably, Dave ran through the roadblock. Then he maneuvered around several other police cars, which proceeded to collide with one another (just like in the movies).

He kept on—through another roadblock, eluding the county sheriff and police from four towns. As I watched the needle of the speedometer hit 110 miles per hour, I felt numb.

Suddenly, all was quiet. We had reached the country. Dave slowed down and shouted, "We made it!"

Just then I heard sirens, and out of nowhere came three police cars. We were surrounded. Again Dave gunned it, but this time he skidded into a gravel driveway and crashed. He yanked me to my feet and ran for a cornfield, dragging me behind. A cop appeared and fired a gun into the air. I collapsed.

Dave was arrested, but the police let me go because I was just an innocent rider. My outraged father picked me up at the police station.

Needless to say, I never went out with Dave again.

The Shock in the Lounge

In the words of Judson, pastor:

Twenty years ago, I was smitten by a fair-skinned, raven-crested beauty, who was also nearly two feet shorter than I.

It was love. True love. It was the kind of love you only dare feel when you are young ... when your heart and soul can absorb the pain and longing that youthful, emotional, and mental instability spawn. It was the kind of love that increases the sales of rock-and-roll love songs and over-the-counter acne medicines.

Yes, this was the love to which I was victim. But I was soon to be doubly victimized. The girl left me. Why she left, I don't know. Perhaps she became jealous of my height and wanted to cut me down to size. In my pain and panic, I lost my head. (Without my head and neck, I would be nearly fourteen inches shorter. I wondered if that would make her like me any better.)

Devastated by her abandonment, wallowing in pain and sorrow, I devised a plan. I decided to make her jealous by using another girl. I would date someone else and make it look like I was falling for her. Jealousy was a powerful emotion, I knew, because I had been jealous of other guys. Jealousy would be the key back into her heart.

Soon I put my plan into action. I met a girl in my psychology class. She was pretty, intelligent, available, and only a little shorter than I. We had our first date, and we had a pretty good time.

In fact, we had a number of pretty good times. I began to feel that if I didn't win my old girlfriend back, it would be nice to keep this new girlfriend in my arms. It seemed like a good alternative, although I really felt guilty

that, at present, I was using this poor, innocent child to get my old girlfriend back.

Well, summer vacation loomed on the scene, and I decided I would let my decision settle out over the summer break. My new girlfriend lived in a different town, so I wouldn't see her over break. In the meantime, I could see my old girlfriend and talk about my new girlfriend in her presence. That way, I could check out the effect of my scheme. It was a good plan, but I still felt bad about using my new girlfriend.

Finally, the semester ended, and it was time to say good-bye to my new girlfriend for the summer. I called her and arranged a meeting at the house where she stayed.

I arrived at her house a few minutes early. She was supposed to come out to the car, but because I was early, I saw no harm in going in and waiting for her in the lounge. No harm, that is, until I entered the room.

There I saw a couple in the corner locked in a rather passionate embrace. I didn't recognize the guy, but the girl was only a little shorter than I was, and from the back, she looked a lot like my new girlfriend. However, it was difficult to make a proper identification when the guy's arms were wrapped around her so tightly. They did a little swoon and turned just enough to give me a side profile.

It was her all right.

Not being a fighting man, I left the room unnoticed and waited in my car. My girlfriend came out ten minutes later, wiping her face with her hanky. I didn't know if she was wiping away sweat or lipstick, and I didn't care. I just said good-bye with a peck on the cheek.

This was too much reality for me to absorb at once. I had come to her house feeling guilty for using her. I left thinking she had been using me too! How could I trust anyone? Especially people shorter than myself!

The summer passed slowly. I didn't see my old girlfriend, but I missed her. I didn't see my new girlfriend either. Every time I thought of her, my stomach got upset.

Two weeks before school began, I made a decision. Once classes started, I would look for a new girl—preferably someone of my own height.

The Girl and Guy Who Went to Court

If you think you've heard everything, hear this. Two high school students from Florida took their courtship to court.

It all started when the guy allegedly stood up the girl on prom night. In response, the girl and her mom sued him for $49.53—the cost of dyed shoes, a hairstyling session, and baby's breath for her hair.

According to the account in *People* magazine, the boy fractured his ankle and claimed he had informed the girl about it five days before the date. The girl countered by saying that when she had talked to him about the injury, he had said the date was still on. The girl went on to note that she took him to court to teach him a lesson, not to win the $49.53.

In this case, I'm not sure which one most deserves to be in the Dating Hall of Shame, but someone sure does. I guess I'll just let the judge be the judge.

Source: "Giving Courtship a New Meaning, a Florida Teen Sues the Date Who Stood Her Up for the School Prom," *People*, 29 May 1989.

THE DATING HALL OF SHAME

The Women Who Oversaw a Court for Lovers

Queen Eleanor, Countess Marie, Countess Isabelle of Flanders, Countess Ermengarde of Narbonne, and a bunch of other twelfth-century ladies get the award for one of the weirdest ideas in the history of romance—a lovers' court. This court did more than settle disputes between lovers; it also told people whether they should love someone or not.

According to Morton Hunt's *The Natural History of Love*, historians have a record of twenty-one cases decided in the "court of love." Here is an example of a case brought before the court:

A klutzy sort of knight asked for the love of a lady. But the lady said she would only give her love to him if he became more worthy. The lady proceeded to teach him how to improve his manners and become more manly, and the knight worked hard at his lessons. There was only one problem. By the time his tutoring was over, the knight had become attracted to someone else.

The lady promptly took the knight to the court of love. The court decided the knight *had* to love her because she had put so much work into improving his manners.

Source: Morton M. Hunt, *The Natural History of Love*, New York: Alfred A. Knopf, 1959.

MORE STUFF

Defeating Yourself

If you're ever tempted to fly off the handle in a fight, I suggest you keep the image in mind of a wrestling match that actually happened in Providence, Rhode Island. One of the wrestlers, a fellow by the name of Pinto, went so wild that somehow he tangled himself up in the ringside ropes. And as he thrashed and struggled to get loose, he accidentally put his shoulders against the mat for three seconds. In other words, while his opponent stood by and watched, he pinned himself and lost the match.

When we get into verbal fights with our girlfriends or boyfriends, it can be very easy to lash out with wild, uncontrollable statements. When we do, we usually find ourselves getting tangled up in our pride and egos. Then we end up doing or saying things that make us look as ridiculous as Pinto, the wrestler who pinned himself. Like poor Pinto, we may end up doing something we never intended. We destroy our relationships, and we defeat ourselves.

Proverbs 13:3 puts it well: "He who guards his lips guards his life, but he who speaks rashly will come to ruin."

In their book, *Between People*, Gerald R. Miller and Mark Steinberg describe several forms of conflict, the most destructive one being what they call "ego conflict." But if they don't mind, I'd rather refer to it as "You're a dweeb!" conflict.

With this form of conflict, emotions run high. People get so fired up, they start bringing in other issues. They dump on each other. They attack their girlfriends or boyfriends personally.

HE: Let's go to a movie tonight.

SHE: What a stupid idea. You *always* suggest the same thing every time we talk about going out. Don't you have any creativity at all?

HE: Well, I wanted to suggest we go to the pool. But every time we go there, you start flirting with other guys. You can be awfully insensitive at times. You're insensitive to me. And you're insensitive to your best friend. Katie told me you are.

A simple disagreement about where to go for a date erupts into an all-out attack on each other's personality. If you can keep conflicts contained to the disagreement at hand, if you can stop them from becoming "You're a dweeb!" conflicts, you have taken a major step.

You'll also avoid making yourself look ridiculous.

CHAPTER 6

THE END

Breaking up is really hard. The pain lingers on. Even a month later, you might see your ex-girlfriend with someone else; and as you watch her move across the room, you take a deep breath, your eyes start to well with tears, and your throat begins to tighten. No, you're not getting all choked up. Actually, your *new* girlfriend is choking you in a jealous rage.

When your relationship comes to an end, you're also bound to hear a lot of advice, some of it good, some of it not. Most likely, one of the things

you'll hear is, "Don't worry about losing your girlfriend. There are still plenty of fish in the sea."

I never did quite understand this piece of advice. For hours, I would lie awake wondering what the amount of fish in the sea had to do with the fact that my ex-girlfriend just compared me to a nocturnal rodent that lives in alleys. Sometimes, I would even wander down the beach and shuffle through the sand along with other people who had recently been dumped by their dates. We would all look into the sea, turn to each other, and say,

"Yup. There are still plenty of fish in the sea."

The good news is that one day, when I was taking a deep whiff of sea air, I suddenly understood the meaning of that expression. What people had been telling me all along is that some things, namely fish, stink almost as bad as my dating life.

When you break up with your boyfriend or girlfriend, another thing people will probably tell you is, "You should part as friends." I agree. I think it is a good idea to remain friends when you end a relationship. As you know, these boy/girl friendships are called "platonic" relationships, in honor of the Greek philosopher Plato.

My theory is that Plato came up with the idea of boy/girl friendships because he had a horrible dating life himself. He may have even worshiped the Greek god of dating disasters—Thaydoomptalatafus (pronounced "They-dumped-a-lot-of-us").

I must admit, however, that I can't blame girls for not going out with a guy like Plato. How would you like to go out to dinner with Plato, hoping for a good conversation, and then have to listen to him say things like, "Ye who affirm that hot and cold or any other two principles are the universe, what is this term that you apply to both of them, and what do you mean when you say that both and each of them 'are'? How are we to understand the word 'are'?"

Plato must have had a lot of Saturday nights by himself to think up all that stuff.

But enough of this. Let's move into the final chapter by looking at ways to make your breaking-up process a foundering mess, and then we'll visit a superhero who rescues doomed relationships.

Getting Dumped Without Novocaine

The Boy's Perspective

1. Become thrilled when your best friend tells you he heard that a cheerleader named Gabrielle has a crush on you.

2. Decide then and there that you're going to break up with your present girlfriend, Ann, who's not a cheerleader.

3. Decide that the nicest way to end the relationship is to avoid Ann and hope she'll get the message.

4. Whenever Ann bicycles to your home, have your entire family run out of the house and pretend they are lawn statues. That way, Ann will think nobody is home.

5. When avoidance doesn't work, drop hints that you are losing interest in your relationship by saying things to your girlfriend like, "Who are you dating these days?"

6. When that doesn't work, show up at Ann's house with blond hairs on your shoulders. (Ann has dark hair.)

7. When that doesn't work, show up at her house with a blond girl on your shoulders.

The Girl's Perspective

1. Act confused when your best friend, Gabrielle, suggests that you break up with Kevin because he's childish.

2. Agree with Gabrielle when she notes that Kevin's most romantic gesture is when he tweeks your nose and shouts, "Got your nose!"

3. Agree with Gabrielle when she notes that Kevin's idea of fun is to open his mouth while eating and shout, "Made you look!"

4. Tell Gabrielle that you don't want to break up because your older sister will probably say, "I told you so. I told you Kevin was no good."

5. Agree with Gabrielle when she notes that you and Kevin don't have puppy love—you have "pit bull love." You're always at each other's throats.

6. Agree with Gabrielle when she notes that "not every dating relationship is meant to last a lifetime. It just feels that way."

7. Agree with Gabrielle when she also notes that you and Kevin "just don't have the right chemistry—except to make a nuclear bomb."

8. Finally become convinced that it's time to end your relationship with Kevin.

9. Bicycle to Kevin's house to tell him about your feelings, but find nobody home.

10. Upon leaving, admire the new lawn statues in the front yard.

11. Later that evening, when you think about facing Saturday night without a date, change your mind and decide you're *not* going to break up with Kevin.

The Boy's Perspective

1. Sitting on the swing on Ann's front porch, run out of things to say.

2. In desperation, grab her nose and shout, "Got your nose!"

3. Wonder why Ann hasn't gotten any of your subtle hints that you want to break up.

4. Decide you must be up front about your feelings.

5. Clear your throat.

6. Mumble.

7. Finally, tell Ann you've decided you want to be able to see other people.

8. When Ann suggests you get a new pair of glasses, tell her, "That's not what I meant by 'wanting to be able to see other people'."

9. Get into a big fight.

10. Try to calm things down by saying you and Ann should pray about your relationship.

11. Feel smug and pious as you pray, "Dear God, help Ann to see what a jerk she is being and that she really is trying to control me too much and that she should be sensitive to my needs and let me have some freedom."

12. Feel righteous anger as Ann prays, "Dear God, help Kevin see that his heart is filled with toxic waste and that he has been awfully cruel the past few weeks, insensitive to my needs, and downright uncharitable and mean."

13. When it's your turn to pray, say, "Dear God, help Ann to see that if she thought about *my* needs and not just *her* needs, then maybe she wouldn't try to dominate my life and tell me how to live when we're barely even dating seriously."

14. Get angry again as Ann prays, "Dear God, help Kevin see that even though he thinks we're barely even dating seriously, he's been giving out a different message for weeks, and he's led me on without ever getting his feelings out in the open."

15. Say amen.

16. Fume.

The Girl's Perspective

1. Tell Gabrielle that you and Kevin broke up yesterday after school—this time for good.

2. Gasp when Gabrielle tells you she already knows you broke up because Kevin called her last night and asked for a date.

3. Gasp again when Gabrielle says that Kevin evidently heard from someone that she had a crush on him.

4. Smile when Gabrielle says that whoever told Kevin she had a crush on him made a big mistake. Actually, she had said, "I'd like to crush Kevin. Preferably with a big rock."

5. After smiling, begin to feel pretty lousy.

6. Tell Gabrielle you feel empty without Kevin.

7. Agree with Gabrielle when she notes that Kevin was just using you, even though he claimed to be interested in your mind.

8. Agree with Gabrielle when she notes that Kevin was more interested in your "don't mind"—your willingness to act as if you don't mind when he treated you like garbage.

9. Even though you agree with everything Gabrielle says, still feel lousy.

10. That night, sit by the phone and wonder if Kevin will call.

11. When the phone finally rings, stare at it.

12. When it's on the fifteenth ring, walk into the kitchen and make a sandwich.

13. When it's on the thirty-second ring, stand by the phone and munch on your sandwich.

14. Pick up the phone on the forty-second ring.

15. Tell the caller, "No, George doesn't live here. You have the wrong number."

16. Stare at the phone for another ten minutes, slowly downing a glass of milk.

17. In a sudden flurry of action, dart for the closet, throw on your coat, and drive to Kevin's house.

18. When the door to Kevin's house opens, rush into the living room hurling aside your coat.

19. When Kevin appears at the top of the staircase, stare up at him with great expectation.

20. Watch as Kevin breaks into a broad smile, says he missed you, and rushes toward you, arms extended.

21. Hold out your arms.

22. When he comes within four feet of you, grab his nose, pinch *hard*, and shout, "Got my nose back!"

23. Turn around and drive home.

24. Learn to get over him.

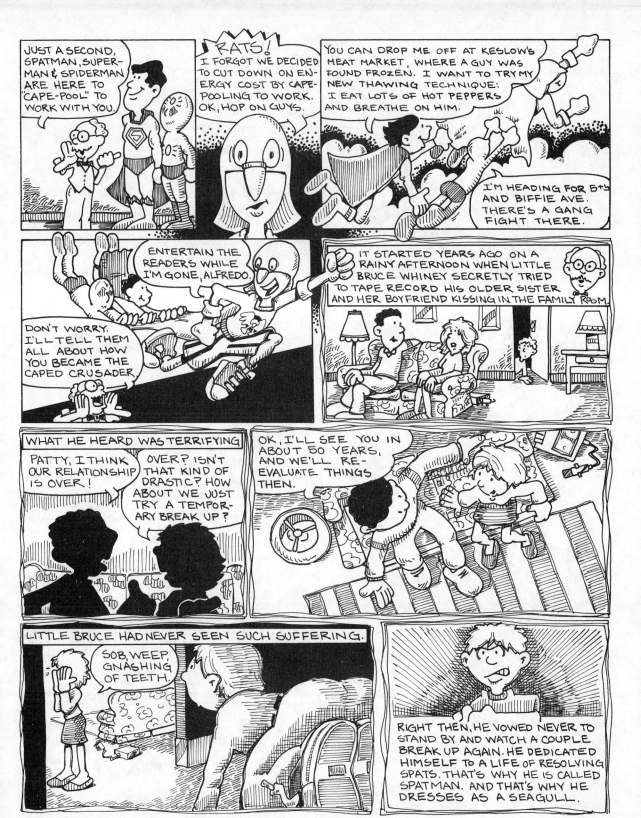

99

A Sure Way to Avoid Breaking Up

Mihailo Tolotos never had the heartbreaking experience of breaking up with a girl. That's because this Greek monk, who died in 1938 at the age of eighty-two, never even *looked* at a female during his entire life.

The day after he was born, Mihailo's mother died, and he was taken to a monastery high in the mountains. Because female wildlife were not allowed in the monastery, Mihailo never even saw a female animal his entire life.

Source: Kevin McFarland, *Incredible!* Hart Publishing Company, 1976.

The Government and Dating

During World War I, U.S. government posters encouraged girls to drop boyfriends who were not willing to enlist in the army.

Source: E. S. Turner, *A History of Courting,* New York: E. P. Dutton, 1955.

The Broken Heart

In 1856, Eliza Emily Donnithorne of Sydney, Australia, was supposed to be married, but her husband-to-be never showed up. Heartbroken, she never left her house for thirty years. She even locked the room where the wedding celebration was

supposed to be held, leaving the cake and decorations in place to rot.

It is believed that her tragedy gave Charles Dickens the idea for his famous Miss Havisham character in his novel, *Great Expectations*.

Source: *Strange Stories, Amazing Facts,* Pleasantville, New York: The Reader's Digest Association, 1976.

Obit Bracelets

In Connecticut in the 1950s, some girls wore "obit bracelets." When a girl broke up with a boy, she added his initials to the bracelet.

Source: Beth L. Bailey, From Front Porch to Back Seat: *Courtship in Twentieth-Century America*, Baltimore: The Johns Hopkins University Press, 1988.

Take Your Breath Away

If you're looking for a way to break off a relationship, writer Marshal Efron has an idea. He suggests that companies produce Scent Re-pellents—chewing gum or mints that make your breath smell foul. Just pop a few mints and you're sure to put an end to any romance. The mints would come in three flavors: onion, garlic, and gym socks.

Source: Randy Cohen and Alexandra Anderson, *Why Didn't I Think Of That?* New York: Fawcett Columbine Books, 1980.

Love Insurance

Some companies have been known to insure the strangest things ... even love relationships. If the love relationship crumbles, the policy-holder collects insur-ance money.

Source: David Wallechinsky and Irving Wallace, *The People's Almanac*, Garden City, New York: Doubleday & Company, 1975.

Devoted Birds

We can learn something about devotion from cranes, those large, graceful birds with the long necks.

George Archibald, a scientist in Wiscon-sin, tells about a sandhill crane that would come to the same road every night. Archi-bald learned from a state trooper that the crane's mate had been killed by a car at that spot. The crane would return every night and stare into the distance, waiting for her mate to come back.

Source: Mark Jerome Walters, *The Dance of Life: Courtship in the Animal Kingdom* , New York: Arbor House, 1988.

IN THEIR OWN WORDS

Upside Down in a Huge Ferris Wheel

In the words of John and Sylvia Ronsvalle, Christian research and service organization directors:

It was the 1960s and the University of Illinois was sponsoring a carnival. The high point of the carnival's midway was a huge Ferris wheel type of ride. It had little round cages that seated two people side-by-side. Using a small steering wheel, the more adventuresome could spin the cage while the Ferris wheel traveled in a huge circle.

John and Sylvia were enjoying the carnival on what might have been called a "date," except that word was not in vogue in the late sixties. But John's face clouded when Sylvia decided not to go on the mega-Ferris wheel.

A truly liberated man, John wanted to reassure Sylvia that she could be a whole human being and didn't need to try to act "feminine." As far as he was concerned, she didn't need to play games by acting nervous and scared. However, Sylvia's reason for not going on the ride had nothing to do with her femininity or lack thereof. It was much simpler than that.

Years ago, her family had taken a vacation to the Smoky Mountains. At first five-year-old Sylvia had a great time riding in the car and taking in the sights. But then they drove deeper into the mountains, following a scenic two-lane road. Sylvia took one look down the sheer drop-off on the side of the road and began screaming at the top of her lungs. She continued screaming until her older sister pushed her head down and sat on her.

Ever since, Sylvia had spent her life as close to the earth as possible. So when John proposed riding the Ferris wheel, she of course charmingly declined.

John did not know about the Smoky Mountain incident, and for some reason this ride was important to him. They took sides and a struggle of wills emerged. After some exchanges, Sylvia weakly consented. She

really, really liked John. And she thought maybe she had changed since she was five.

John was smiling as they waited in line, but Sylvia looked as though she were about to be locked in prison. And that's what the small barred cages looked like too—a prison. Finally, the carnival worker opened the door to their cage. Shaking visibly, Sylvia stepped in and immediately fastened her safety strap.

How many times in one minute can you say, "Don't let this thing go around"? You'd be surprised how quickly that phrase can be repeated under certain circumstances. Sylvia said it many, many times before John even got in. The carnival worker looked doubtingly at John, but he merely smiled back reassuringly.

The door shut. John belted himself in. The Ferris wheel rotated one station, and Sylvia groaned. Then John noticed that where the steering wheel should have been, there was only a one-inch metal pole and a large, sharp-edged bolt for holding the wheel in place. With no wheel, they couldn't control how many times their cage turned circles while the Ferris wheel went around.

John looked at Sylvia. Sylvia looked at John. Sylvia's face went white with sheer horror. And John no longer looked so self-assured.

"Don't let this go around," she croaked, clearly desperate. John grabbed the end of the bare metal tube with both hands just as the Ferris wheel lurched into motion.

Every muscle within Sylvia tensed. Not speaking, not moving, she fixed her eyes on John's hands, which were turning white from the effort to keep the cage from rotating uncontrollably.

They survived the compulsory number of Ferris wheel rotations in intense silence. But by some malicious turn of fate, their cage stopped on the very top, halfway up on the Ferris wheel's journey. Also, because John had succeeded in keeping the cage from turning at all, their feet were now above their heads.

"I have to let it turn once, Sylvia," John said, using a calm, measured voice.

Sylvia had no strength left. "Can you catch it again?"

Neither one was trying to impress the other anymore.

"I don't know," John said, "but you have to get my handkerchief out of my pocket because my hand is starting to bleed.

"I can't move," Sylvia said.

"Please try."

She carefully, carefully reached behind, ever so slowly, without disturbing their precarious position in the slightest, and retrieved the white handkerchief sticking out of John's back pocket.

Through the heroic strength that people say is at our disposal in desperate situations, John succeeded in getting the cage right-side-up, allowing it to move only one-half turn. Now they had a panoramic view of the flat Illinois campus at night. The Ferris wheel jerked forward again.

It stopped once more. And this time their cage had them facing the ground, spread out hundreds of feet below. Unsuspecting merrymakers wandered to and fro as a new problem presented itself.

Sylvia looked down at this unique perspective and said flatly, "I'm going to throw up."

John was convinced that they had grown beyond the game-playing stage in their relationship. He frantically searched through his psychology training but no appropriate strategy leaped to mind.

"Please don't," he begged.

"I can't help it."

"It will get on those people's heads."

"I can't help it."

"It might splash back up on us as it hits the cage."

"I wish this ride were over," Sylvia moaned.

The Ferris wheel lurched again, and they came into the platform upside down. The carnival worker roughly righted the cage. It took John several seconds to uncramp his hands from the steering wheel pole. Sylvia was shaking as she stepped out on the platform.

John and Sylvia eventually got married in spite of this disastrous date. And years later, John let Sylvia fulfill a childhood fantasy when he took her to Disneyland for the first time. This time she loved the rides, especially since John let *her* handle the flight controls on Dumbo.

The Frenchman

In the words of Meg, counselor:

So you want to hear about a disastrous date?

I suppose I could tell you about the time I was on crutches and nearly fell over trying to avoid contact during the "goodnight kiss" moment of the date.

Or maybe I could tell you about the time my date left to get popcorn at the beginning of the movie and never returned. He decided to watch the feature next door.

Then again, maybe I should tell you about the time I reached out to hold my date's hand and ended up holding the hand of my girlfriend's date instead.

Actually, though, I think the time I'll tell you about is my first date with Jean. ("Jean" is a French name pronounced the same as "John.") After dinner, we went to my house. Because Jean was French, he brought along some French music tapes from his car.

We were talking in our family room, the music playing softly in the background, when Jean turned to me and quietly said, "If I could, I would take you to a place where the ocean meets the shore, where the sun dances on the waves as it sets in the distance."

Wow! My face started to flush, and I could feel chills running up and down my spine. My heart was racing. I thought, *It's true. Frenchmen are more sensitive and romantic than the English. This is really incredible!*

He continued with his gentle wooing: "Days would seem endless as we walked along the beaches hand in hand."

I was starting to feel faint. Now I knew why French mademoiselles used to come to balls equipped with fans. I needed air. I tried to keep breathing calmly as I looked into his eyes.

Then he said, "But I'm a woman, and women cannot make these things come to be."

My heart stopped and my face dropped. "You're a what?"

I stared at him, and he just sat there smiling at me. He didn't blink. He didn't even move a muscle. And then I realized. He'd been translating the words to the French song playing in the background!

THE DATING HALL OF SHAME

The Man Who Made a Dumb Promise

The time was the Middle Ages, and a man had lost his heart to a woman. But the woman was anything but impressed. In fact, she hated the thought of this man singing her praises everywhere he went.

The lady finally told the man she would love him, but under only one condition. He must agree to obey all of her commands. A wildly devoted and foolish lover, the man agreed. Then the lady promptly gave her first command. She ordered him to stop trying to win her love, and to stop talking to other people about how wonderful she was.

In other words, the only way he could keep her love was if he obeyed her command and stopped loving her. It was a sneaky way to get him out of her hair.

Source: Andreas Capellanus, *The Art of Courtly Love,* New York: Frederick Ungar Publishing Company, 1959.

The Men Who Told Half-Truths about Half Sisters

If anyone ever tells you the Bible is boring, tell them they're crazy. How can it be boring when there are wonderfully wacky people

like Abraham and Isaac running around in it? Abraham and Isaac are both prime candidates for the Dating Hall of Shame.

The craziness all started when Abraham and his wife, Sarah, decided to take a trip to Egypt. They loaded up the mini-van or mini-camel or whatever they drove back then, made sure they didn't leave the iron on, and took off. But as they neared Egypt, Abraham got a bit nervous. You see, Sarah was extremely beautiful, most likely a prom queen, and Abraham was afraid that Egyptian men would want to date her. They might even want to add her to their harems. Because Abraham and Sarah were married, however, an Egyptian man would have to kill Abraham before he

could add Sarah to his harem.

Abraham thought about this ... a lot. So he concocted one of those sneaky little lies—a half-truth. He told Sarah to tell everyone she was just his sister. That way, if somebody wanted to add Sarah to his harem, he could do it without killing Abraham. Abraham justified this lie in his mind because Sarah actually was his "half-sister." In other words, they had the same father but different mothers.

Sure enough, when they got to Egypt, the Pharaoh flipped out over Sarah and immediately made plans to add her to his harem. The Bible doesn't say if they actually went out on any dates, and it doesn't say whether Abraham played the role of the pesky brother by listening in on Sarah's phone calls. But it does say Pharaoh eventually discovered that Sarah was really Abraham's wife.

When he confronted Abraham with the discovery, Abraham probably responded with the Hebrew word for "Oops." (For more information on "Oops," see the Dating Hall of Shame in chapter 4.) Enraged, Pharaoh kicked Abraham and Sarah out of their rooms in the Holiday Inn and told them to get lost.

You'd think Abraham would have learned his lesson after that. But many years later, when he and Sarah moved to Gerar, Abraham tried the trick again. Fearing that other men would kill him for his wife, he told everyone Sarah was his sister. This time, a ruler named Abimelech fell for the beautiful Sarah and began to woo her. But his "woo" changed to "whoa!" when God sent a message to him in a dream. (Dreams are cheaper than using a fax machine.) God revealed to Abimelech that Abraham and Sarah were married, so Abimelech promptly sent the couple on their way.

Like father, like son. Many years later, while Abraham's son Isaac was traveling in

Gerar, he became afraid that some nasty man would kill him and marry his beautiful wife, Rebekah. So he scratched his head, thought for a little bit, and recalled that his father had a nifty trick for situations like this.

"Oh, yeah, I remember now," he said to himself. "Yo Rebekah! While we're in Gerar, you'll pretend you're my sister. OK?"

So Isaac and Rebekah continued their travels in Gerar, where they met a fellow named Abimelech. (This was *not* the same Abimelech that Abraham encountered.) Struck by Rebekah's beauty, Abimelech made plans to add her to his harem. That is, he made plans until he spotted Isaac and Rebekah kissing on the park bench.

Oops.

Source: *Holy Bible: New International Version*, the book of Genesis, chapters 12, 20, and 26, Zondervan Bible Publishers, Grand Rapids, Michigan.

One Day in Music Class

It happened at the end of my junior year in college, just a few months before I married Nancy. I was sitting in Music Appreciation class, having a real hard time appreciating the music of Johann Sebastian Bach. I was tired.

The next thing I knew, I saw myself in a huge cathedral. Bach's music, which seemed pretty boring a few seconds earlier, suddenly sounded intensely emotional. I was standing in the cathedral's balcony, staring down on a sea of white dresses. The floor of the cathedral was overflowing with brides, all of them slowly moving toward the balcony. I was in a black tuxedo. I didn't look behind me, but I knew I was standing in the midst of a thousand other bridegrooms. I remember looking down into the crowd of brides and thinking, *Nancy's out there.*

Then, as I slowly turned, I sensed the presence of Nancy beside me as we started to walk upwards to God. It was an incredible experience, especially for someone like myself who doesn't have many emotional religious experiences.

But the more amazing thing happened a week later in the same class. The teacher played the same piece by Bach. Only this time she added a statement that made me jump in my seat. She said Bach had hoped that this particular music would get the listener to picture the image of Christ marrying his bride—the church.

Evidently, what I had seen in my daydream was much more than just my own wedding. I had viewed the marriage between Christ and ourselves — the church.

The image of Christ as the groom and the church as his bride is powerfully presented throughout the New Testament. It also seems to be an image that God enjoys giving to ordinary people—people like me and a nun by the name of Christine.

In his book, *The Signature of Jesus* (Old Tappan, New Jersey: Revell, 1988), Brennan Manning tells how Christine was alone in her room one night, praying and reflecting on the image of Christ as her husband. The next thing she knew, she was in a huge ballroom filled with people. She was sitting along the wall when a handsome man took her by the hand and began swirling her around the room. Everybody else stopped to stare as Christine and the man danced, perfectly matched, never missing a step. She had never felt more loved and alive than at that moment. Suddenly she noticed the wounds in the man's hands. And then she knew she was dancing with Jesus.

When the dance ended, Jesus leaned close to Christine and spoke a few simple, but important words. He said, "Christine, I'm wild about you."

I have a reason for mentioning this image of Christ as bridegroom and lover. I even have a reason for including it in a chapter about breaking up. When a dating relationship comes crashing to an end, it's easy to

feel totally alone, deserted, and unloved. In those times, it's comforting to know that no matter how shattered our love life may be, Jesus still loves us. He is as devoted to us as a bridegroom.

I know it's easy to say, "Don't worry. Jesus still loves you. He still cares." Words like these often sound shallow when we're hurting. That's why we need more than words. We need a relationship with Jesus. By "relationship," I mean a lasting oneness, like husband and wife. When Jesus is that real to us, he can help in ways we cannot even imagine.

Guys probably have a hard time relating to the idea that they are the bride of Jesus. So for them, I offer another image. Think of Jesus as a friend who is as real to you as the friend sitting next to you in class.

To show how comforting this image can be, I leave you with another story from Manning's book, *The Signature of Jesus*. Manning tells of a woman whose father was dying. Upon her request, a priest agreed to visit her father.

The priest approached the bedside of the dying man, and there he noticed an empty chair placed beside the bed. The priest asked the man if he had just had a visitor, and the man looked a little embarrassed. Then the dying man explained that he had always had trouble praying to God until a friend suggested a solution. The friend said that prayer is a conversation with God, and that it sometimes helps to talk with God by setting up an empty chair and imagining that Jesus is sitting in it, just chatting with you.

The man asked if the priest thought it was weird to pray with an empty chair beside his bed, and the priest assured him it wasn't.

A few days later, the man's daughter informed the priest that her father had died.

The priest asked if he had died peacefully, and she told him that her father had been smiling and joking when she left him that afternoon. When she returned over an hour later, he was dead.

However, there was one strange thing, added the daughter. Her father had died with his head resting on an empty chair beside his bed.

The man did not die alone. He died with his head in the lap of Jesus. Our Lord is that real. Christ is that comforting.

A Vaccine For Dating

In the 1950s, "polio" was a dread word. The disease struck without warning and without rhyme or reason. It paralyzed victims, leaving many crippled for life. I remember hearing a person tell about waking up one morning to see his brother carried off to the hospital. His back had bent violently backwards, turning him into a human *U*.

With scenes like that etched in the minds of millions, you can imagine the reception that Jonas Salk received when he created a vaccine for polio. I have heard it said that during the avalanche of publicity following this discovery, a reporter asked Salk whether it was frustrating to face failure after failure before discovering a vaccine that worked.

Salk told the reporter it wasn't hard to cope because he had never failed. Each attempt at creating a vaccine was not a failure, he said. Each attempt was a crucial step, a necessary step, that eventually led to a workable vaccine.

Wouldn't it be nice if we could maintain such an attitude in our love life? Wouldn't it be nice if we could come away from a broken relationship without feeling like a failure? Wouldn't it be nice if we could think of every relationship as a vital step leading to the ultimate relationship that we may have someday with a spouse?

In other words, wouldn't it be nice if we *learned* something from our relationships, no matter how broken they appear?

Dating is an adventure. And the best way to approach adventure is with an enthusiasm that shatters the fear of failure.

That is known as having the Right Stuff.

THERE'S EVEN MORE STUFF

You've made it. You've read this book, and now you have the credentials to be officially certified as a "Wrong Stuff-er." You now know how to wreak havoc on dates, how to reach astounding levels of clumsiness, and how to trip over your tongue with ease.

Hopefully, you've also learned to laugh at your blunders.

In conclusion, I leave you with a warning. After you have perfected your skills in creating disastrous dates, you might find yourself saying, "What else is there? I've done it all. I've been as awkward as humanly possible. I've said the goofiest things while trying to be romantic. I've fouled up just about every aspect of my dates. What's left? Where's the challenge?"

For those who have reached this pinnacle of Wrong Stuffness, I have good news. As you leave the world of dating, there are other worlds to bungle your way through. For instance, there are wedding ceremonies. Yes, wedding ceremonies. What an ideal place for disaster to strike.

If you don't believe me, then take a look at this final installment of "In Their Own Words." It's living proof that there is hope. There are many areas left where the Wrong Stuff can be displayed in all its glory.

The Catastrophic Wedding

In the words of Wilmer Zehr, photographer:

A number of years ago, I was scheduled to photograph a wedding, which was to begin at 1:00 P.M. As was standard practice, I arrived thirty minutes before the scheduled time. But as I parked in the parking lot, I noticed that people were leaving. Something did not seem right.

I ran up to the church to find an empty sanctuary. I heard voices in the basement, so I went downstairs. The people there seemed to be celebrating a funeral, not a wedding. People were in tears, including the bride and

read 11:00 instead of 1:00.

Were they in tears because I was late? That was just one of many things. First, one of the bridesmaids smoking in the dressing room burned a hole in the bride's veil. Next, when the flowers arrived, they discovered that they were for a different wedding. The flower count was off and so were the colors. Then, after they decided to go ahead with the flowers they had, the wedding proceeded (without a photographer). As the bride and father were going down the aisle, the person who was positioning the train-length veil stepped on it, pulling it off when the bride was halfway down the aisle.

The next problem occurred during the ceremony. It was very hot and humid, and under the nervous pressure of the day, the groom fainted and had to be carried out to be revived before the ceremony continued.

When the wedding party arrived in the reception hall, they discovered that the top two layers of the cake had slid off and hit the floor because of the heat.

We arranged to restage most of the pictures, but of course it wasn't quite the same. When the bride and groom picked up their proofs, however, they were able to laugh about it all. And to my knowledge, they lived happily ever after.

ding. I checked my appointment card. Yes, it said 1:00. When I began to check what was going on, I discovered they had forgotten to put another "1" on the time. It should have